Lord and Scoutmaster

Tales of High Adventure Reflecting the Natures of Boys and Men and of the King of Kings

by

Karl M. Duff

© Copyright 1990 — Karl M. Duff

All rights reserved. This book is protected under the copyright laws of the United States of America. This book may not be copied or reprinted for commercial gain or profit. Short quotations or occasional page copying for personal or group study is permitted and encouraged. Permission will be granted upon request. Unless otherwise identified, Scripture quotations are from The New American Standard Version of the Bible.

Companion Press
P.O. Box 351
Shippensburg, PA 17257

ISBN 1-56043-457-0

For Worldwide Distribution
Printed in the U.S.A.

Contents

Chapter		Page
	Dedication	iv
	The Boy	v
	Preface	vii
	The Spirit of Scouting	x
1	The Call of Scouting	1
2	A Scout's Reproof	5
3	Taking Lessons from a Scout	9
4	Scoutmaster's Luck	15
5	Tasting Some Fruit	21
6	Fixing Bill's Teeth	27
7	High Adventure — Eastern Style	31
8	Scouts Will Be Boys	37
9	Christmas Trees — 1973	43
10	Not an Eagle	45
11	I Shall Supply Your Needs	51
12	Gold Nugget Camping	55
13	A Family in Grief	59
14	A Lesson in Obedience	63
15	Boys Without Fathers	71
16	An Adventure in Forgiveness — Part I	79
17	An Adventure in Forgiveness — Part II	83
18	An Adventure in Forgiveness — Part III	87
19	Larry	89
20	Parade Ground Miracle	93
21	ADD 659	97
22	Helping Hands	99
23	Scoutmaster's Son	101
24	Patterns of Providence	107
25	Law of Generations	115
26	Closing Accounts	121
27	Nature	129
28	Salvation	135
29	Strength Out of Adversity	139
30	Seeds of Baden-Powell	143
31	The Nowhere Road	147
	Epilogue	153

*To Gretchen, my nourisher and healer
...who has been
Scout-widowed nearly 600 nights.*

The Boy

Young boy running, playing, dreaming
in his world of reverie.
Bare feet tripping, senses listening
to a childhood melody.

Shining skies at end of day
golden sunlight fading, gone.
Hear the call and, quickly running,
soon he's round the bend and
...home

Young man growing, dreaming, learning
tunes of different melody.
New to senses reaching, searching
'yound the bounds of family.

Shining eyes and world are calling,
muting now the songs of home.
Hear the call and, quickly running,
soon he's round the bend and
...gone.

Karl Duff

Preface

Why has Boy Scouts of America been so successful? Since its establishment in 1910, Boy Scouting has been the most popular and successful youth program America has known. Even in the face of modern affluence and the loss of much of America's pioneer mentality and her wilderness, as well as competing organized sports, Boy Scouting remains popular, though not without modern-day stresses and challenges. Why is this so? What draws boys to adventure and what draws men to lead them? What are the legacies that are placed in their lives that cause them all to count Scouting as one of their most rewarding activities of life — and one with the best memories?

The answers are complex and probably don't simplify convincingly. Life experiences do not easily distill into doctrine. But there are certain things which I feel explain Scouting's success. They involve relationships and manhood. If possible, I would like to see the true principles of Scouting's success conveyed to other men and, through them, to other boys.

This book is an attempt to capture the ingredients of my experiences in many different boys' lives in Scouting in a manner which illustrates the recurrent themes and lessons I've seen. I have highlighted the lessons which have meant much to me personally. They contain information which is relevant to me but which may or may not be relevant to others. They leave considerable interpretation to the reader, but hopefully convey some of my convictions as well.

It may be, however, that transferring the actual precepts of Scouting is not possible except through living Scouting with others. Hence, these stories may accomplish only what they appear, superficially, designed to do: form an inspirational story book which will entertain and inspire readers in the manner of camp fire stories. Possibly some, though, will be drawn to enlist in Scouting and discover more for themselves! Perhaps some will even become heavily involved in helping boys. The stories you will read are all true (except the last one, which was heard at a camp fire when I was a Tenderfoot Scout!). Through these actual experiences, the reader may gain some appreciation as to why Scouting has such strong influences on boys and why it has had a strong influence on me!

Central to the whole case is my belief that Scouting is based on the scriptural principles of the Bible and that God reveals Himself in the lives of men and boys who pursue His precepts (John 14:21, Heb. 11:6). The twelve Scout Laws all derive from the admonitions of the God of Israel through the prophets of the Old Testament and through the teachings, character and example of the Lord Jesus Christ. They teach faithfulness, obedience and living one's life for others. They state the existence of God and the need to worship Him. In the same manner that God gives His children a free choice to keep or to violate His precepts and to experience the consequent blessings or curses, so also Scouting teaches standards and gives plenty of freedom to leaders and Scouts to "do their best" in keeping the Scout Law or not. Scouting tends to highlight our behavior against a standard and helps to illustrate how painfully like the children of Israel we are in falling short of the mark.

But the key feature that builds and predominates throughout Boy Scouting is relationships. Until boys reach the age of 11, they aren't generally capable of building and maintaining relationships outside the family. Until then, boys draw their lives out of their own families and invest little in the lives of others. Friends they have prior to that time are "playmates," and many of us can't recall playmates we had before that age. Scouting engages and encourages boys to grow in this area at precisely the age at which it becomes possible, by establishing group goals and organizing the activities to attain them. Patrol activities and the tasks of camping are totally different in their demands upon Scouts than are the activities of younger Cub Scouts. They are life-related. Teamwork is needed. Boys must respond to the demands of the activities if they want food, shelter and good feelings. As they respond and invest in their Scouting relationships, the capacities of those relationships also grow.

Involved also is the process of "calling out" and affirming boys into manhood at about the age of puberty, as highlighted by Gordon Dalby in his book, *Healing the Masculine Soul*. Many primitive societies and some modern ones, including that of the Jews, provide a tradition of men "calling out" boys from their mothers into a process of training and growth with other boys under the tutelege of their fathers and other men. Boy Scouting tends to provide the same type of awareness training and affirming experience for boys at this age, thus perhaps fulfilling a true need that boys have and substituting for what has gradually been lost to Western societies.

Ultimately, the measure of a man is in his capacity to do right and give on behalf of others (i.e., to do justly and to love mercy — Micah 6:8). It is response to the demands of Scouting, more than any secular activity available today to boys outside the home, that builds this capacity in young men. Other activities such as sports, music, drama, debate, etc., which also compete for a boy's time, don't compare with Scouting in their contribution to the *life-support capacity* of a boy's character. Today many families are finding, too late, that they pursued the wrong development areas in their sons' formative years and that life-giving/load-bearing capacities are missing in their sons' characters.

Why is this important, especially today? Because the demands of marriage, employment and citizenship require this capacity. They require faithfulness and perseverance. Statistics tell us that these things are in increasingly short supply among our nation's men. Boys and men have been encouraged to pour out their manhood on the ground, "streams of water in the street" (Prov. 5:16) in self-indulgence, sexual promiscuity and material values. The American family, for which men are chiefly responsible, is failing because men are failing.

Scouting is one of the last effective secular institutions for building manhood in young men today because, through the thrill of adventure and the forge of trials, it enables them to find victory under the demands of true life-supporting relationships and principles.

The Spirit of Scouting

Scout Oath or Promise

On my honor, I will do my best
To do my duty to God and my country
and to obey the Scout Law;
To help other people at all times,
To keep myself physically strong,
mentally awake and morally straight.

Scout Law

A Scout is:

- TRUSTWORTHY
- LOYAL
- HELPFUL
- FRIENDLY
- COURTEOUS
- KIND
- OBEDIENT
- CHEERFUL
- THRIFTY
- BRAVE
- CLEAN
- REVERENT

1

The Call of Scouting

"...the gifts and the calling of God are irrevocable."
Romans 11:29

It is hard to say when the call of Scouting took its first firm hold on me. My memories contain many vivid Scouting scenes, dating back to my candlelight initiation ceremony into Cub Scouts at the age of nine. I remember the awe I felt in that dark room when I first took the oath of "trying to do my best" before hosts of witnesses. That awe took on even grander nature when, graduating at the age of 12 into Boy Scouts, I first came into the meeting hut of my new troop and saw a full-length alligator mounted on the wall! What a wonderful place of mystery and adventure! I recall campouts, skill contests, games, singing and other activities that were fun for reasons I never thought about. I was accomplishing something that seemed to be important and having fun with other boys. On occasion there were trials of injury, close calls, nights in the rain or fatigue so great we could think only of climbing into our sleeping bags at the end of the day (a boy's most practical means of escape). But even disasters quickly came into the general context of "fun."

No doubt my recollections are not actually as things were. Even then memories seemed to be frequently unreliable and from time to time there were scenes of fishing holes and campsites that seemed perplexingly different when next visited, sometimes the following year. Things never looked quite the same the next time around. But the memories had a power all their own. They seemed to prevail over what our eyes told us. The scenes of our memory were really "real" — the present was somehow out of place, missing something we relived in our memories. There was also a mysterious chemistry between our memories and our relationships, memories being inextricably tied to those who share in them. Boys who had shared an experience had a special bond. Those who had not shared could not participate afterward in nourishing the legends of our adventures. What powerful bonding was forged through our trials! Witness any man revisiting the scenes of his childhood or friendships which survive the battlefield. Past adventures, the ghosts of dead campfires — scenes of our own personal life history were powerful realities in my Boy Scouting experience, and imagination seemed to be a full-time companion of reality.

Stories told at campfires seem also to transform through a boy's power of imagination into reality of the first order. Eyes of werewolves seem to stare from the bushes. The wind seems to carry the voice of the "Man with the Golden Arm" through the night and attempts at sleep are constantly interrupted by each rustling leaf or snapping twig. Boys seem to enjoy terror in company with each other as part of their appetite for adventure. Stories also convey life principles better than any other form of instruction, and the campfire story I remember most vividly is one I have repeated myself at many other campfires since, "The Story of the Nowhere Road." I first heard this tale at Scout Camp when I was 13 years old (see the closing chapter of this book).

Shortly after I joined the Scouts, my folks moved and I lost the opportunity to attend Scout Camp with my troop. As a compromise, my mother arranged for me to attend "provisional" Scout Camp on my own for a week at Camp Parsons, still the "star" of Boy Scout camps in the Puget Sound area. My mother was as new to it as I was, and after having done her best to get me situated and oriented at camp, she drove off, leaving me alone. I went about 100 feet toward my designated campsite and got lost! I burst into tears and stood there crying until a boy on the camp staff came up to help me. He was about 16 years old, but seemed years older in maturity and knowledge as he helped me to my campsite. I was filled with admiration and respect for this boy who had helped in my hour of need and think I must have viewed him with something akin to worship every time I saw him afterward. I suppose I attributed things to camp staffers which were far beyond the truth, but the lasting lesson given to me was the power of even the slightest helping hand to transform a young boy's attitudes. I am still grateful to that unknown Scout.

My first Scout hike took us out of the downtown Scout hut and a mile or two out into the country to a place called "Camp 40" in Edmonds, Washington. As the new boy in the troop, I was given a large bucket, the community cooking pot, to carry in my pack. Equipment was crude in 1948 and I didn't even have one of the new Trapper Nelson packboards that were becoming popular, which placed a protective canvas web between a person's back and the contents of his packsack. All I had was an Army-surplus bag with straps, and that big pot rubbed my back raw by the time we reached camp. I was much the wiser after that trip, but still totally unprepared for my first hike of major proportions on my second visit to Camp Parsons the following summer.

Summer camp was a two-week experience in my youth, and at Camp Parsons the first four days of the second week were devoted to hikes into the Olympic Mountains within Olympic National Forest and National Park. I signed up for the "Three Rivers" hike, which leads up the Quilcene River, crosses the mountains to the Dungeness River, and then leads over Constance Pass to descend the Dosewallops River. The day we started our trip one of the camp trucks broke down, so they had only one vehicle with which to truck the various hike groups to their starting points. Consequently, to save time they dropped us all off at points a considerable distance from the trailheads. The Three Rivers group was dropped off near the main highway to walk some additional 6-8 miles up a hot, dusty road to reach the transition from logged and burned-over timberland to the cool tall timber of the National Forest. It was mid-afternoon when we reached there and had lunch. We younger Scouts thought we were exhausted and unable to go any further, but with the rest and refreshment of lunch and the commencement of a cooler walk in the woods, we carried on another four or five miles to our point of real exhaustion and our shelter for the night. While we lay helpless, the group leaders put together a good meal for us, and I was amazed to see another of these 16-year-old camp staffers haul a 17-pound watermelon out of his pack to share with us! That helped to give my exhaustion some new perspective! We did our cleanup chores and crawled into our precious sleeping bags inside the shelter just as it was getting dark and starting to rain. What a secure, vital feeling of contentment I had! The rain on the shelter roof was music to my ears.

At that moment another Scouting party from Camp Parsons arrived, having got an even later start than we. They had no dinner. The problem was that there was not enough room in the shelter for two parties and it was another two miles up the trail to the next shelter. After a short conference, our hike leaders told us the bad news. We had to get up, repack everything and hike up the trail another two miles in the dark! By now the rain was pouring down! One cannot imagine our consternation! Within a short while, it turned to despair. In the pouring rain, all the flashlights in the party of 17 were soon reduced to one, given to the hike leader. Slipping and falling down in the mud in the pitch dark, we wondered bitterly how we had got trapped into this. How stupid we were to have volunteered! Most of us were crying. We swore that if we ever got out of this alive, we would never go on another hike.

Then, when we thought surely it couldn't get any worse, word was passed down the line that the hike leader thought he had missed the next shelter in the dark. It was off to the side on a short spur trail. If so, it was another two miles of upgrade to the next campsite, where there was no shelter at all. It looked like we were to spend the whole night out in the rain. One simply cannot describe the hopelessness and despair. We went mechanically through the motions of putting one foot in front of the other, falling down and getting up, soaking wet and covered with mud. How would it all end?

Sometime between 10:00 p.m. and 11:00 p.m. we arrived at the shelter. We hadn't missed it after all. We perfunctorily threw our sleeping bags down on the dry dirt floor and slept the sleep of the totally exhausted.

The next morning dawned grey and cool. The rain had stopped and we had a good breakfast. Our bodies seemed to have healed somewhat and our hike leaders informed us that we had only 5 ½ miles to go this day because of our extraordinary effort the day before. Before we knew it, we were halfway up "Poop Out Drag," a notorious steep grade of two miles that was reputed to have ruined the days of many Scouts who had climbed it in the hot sun. It seemed surprisingly easy! Then we reached the top, Camp Mystery, right at timberline, and I got my first glimpse of the alpine mountains. It held little tarns of clear water, hillocks of heather and flowers scattered between patches of snow and huge granite boulders, rugged ridges of rock against the sky! We strolled through it all. A marmot shrilled his high-pitched whistle and ducked beneath a rock. This was beautiful! I was transported into another world. In an instant, all of my attitudes of the previous day disappeared. I was hooked and can still remember the moment I realized it!

This and other experiences kept me in Scouting through high school until I became an Eagle Scout just before my 17th birthday. Shortly thereafter I joined the Naval Reserve, started college and embarked upon new adventures leading, ultimately, to a Navy career. Four years after entering active duty with the U.S. Navy, I married and then joined the local Methodist Church Boy Scout Troop, Troop 304, in Belmont, Massachusetts, signing on as Assistant Scoutmaster in 1962.

I do not know why this seemed a good idea at the time. Undoubtedly, I wanted to spend some time in the New England countryside. I probably had a desire to relive some of my prior Scouting experiences and to share them with boys. There was probably a desire to test and "show off" some of my skills, and also some altruistic motive in seeking to "put back into Scouting" some of the benefits I had derived. Little did I know of the new adventures upon which this was to lead me; still less did I realize that I was being led, educated and trained by another Scoutmaster far greater than any I had ever perceived!

2

A Scout's Reproof

"All discipline for the moment seems not to be joyful, but sorrowful; yet to those who have been trained by it, afterwards it yields the peaceful fruit of righteousness"

Heb. 12:11

I had a painful and pointed lesson taught to me as a Scout which takes a place in the scheme both of Scouting and of God's work in my life. Although it occurred when I was a boy, it has only been as an adult that I have been able to see the tremendous truth of the principles which were illustrated and that they focused upon deep-rooted problems in me with which God had to deal.

On another of the Scout summer camp hike trips into the Olympic Mountains, I signed up for a climb of Mt. Anderson, the 4th highest peak in the Olympics. It was a fairly rugged trip, with a long approach hike, some extensive rock scrambling and glacier traverses before the actual climb of the peak — which proved more complicated than anticipated because of our getting lost in the fog!

The main difficulty of the trip for me, however, was the assistant hike leader. He was 28 years old and had just been discharged from the U.S. Army after approximately 10 years of service. He was an overbearing bully who passed himself off as an expert in everything, even though it seemed to me that most of the boys in the group knew more about what was going on than he did and we spent quite a bit of our time helping him. For the most part this was well handled by our leader who, again, was about 17 years old and really did know what he was doing. But the ex-sergeant seemed to use his loud bragging and bullying to cover his weaknesses and to indulge some attitudes he had not resolved or left behind with the Army. He also complained a lot, finding fault with everything, and generally made the trip miserable for us.

The weather was poor for most of the trip, but we successfully made the climb and had descended the Dosewallops River trail to within four miles of the end of the road on the fourth night of our trip when we experienced an accident around the campfire. A pot of boiling water tipped over, spilling its contents onto three of us. I was one of the three, but did not get very much of it on my leg and thought little of it. The same was true of a second boy. The third person, who received the greater part of the spill, was the ex-sergeant. He immediately went into hysteria, asserting the most horrible levels of pain and injury. We raised his pant leg and could see that his skin had been reddened to about the same levels as the other two of us, although over a broader area, affecting about two thirds of his lower leg. Despite the efforts of our hike leader to calm him down and bring things into perspective, he soon declared that he would be unable to hike out.

It was not long before the hike leader was calling for volunteers to walk out to the ranger station at the end of the road for a stretcher with which to carry out our large ex-sergeant, who must have weighed close to 200 pounds. I could hardly believe my ears. Was our hike leader falling for this masquerade? How could anyone believe for a moment that this grown man could not walk out to the road on his own in his condition? How could anyone support such a fraud and require that 14 and 15 year-old boys carry him out, in addition to carrying out our own gear? Our hike leader was apparently buying the story, or was unwilling to go against the bullying pleadings of the older man. Early the next morning, off went several of the boys along with our hike leader, taking out their own packs and returning with a stretcher. But I was not buying any part of it. I was not volunteering to do anything I did not have to do for this miserable piece of humanity.

This created quite a bit of conflict within me. I had the strength to volunteer to help, and even had some urging to do so, mainly for the sake of recognition as being identified with those who were helping. I seemed to know that it was the right thing to do, but I also held fast to the idea that it was not right for the strongest man in the group to perpetuate such a fraud on us! I knew, without any doubt whatsoever, that he was perfectly capable of walking and that he probably knew it himself, also. So I sat around in camp while the other volunteers hiked the extra eight miles and brought in the stretcher.

Then we carried him out to the road. We hiked four miles, each of us taking turns on a corner of the stretcher and carrying approximately 50 pounds of dead weight in our hands over roots, rocks and the twists and turns of trail involved. We all knew, though, that the difficulties of carrying him out on this good trail would greatly magnify when we gained the roadway and were transported to the washout! This was the two-mile section of washed-out road we had first slogged through to start our trip, seven miles below the ranger station. It was a veritable quagmire of fallen logs, rocks, small streams, mud and sand which had resulted from the flooding of the river that spring. Everyone knew in his heart we would be unable to carry the ex-sergeant's heavy weight once we reached these obstacles. All the while we continued to listen to our hero's charade of pain and self-sacrifice, describing his suffering as he lay on the stretcher! We were exhausted in every way by the time we reached the ranger station.

After a brief rest, we were transported by truck down to the washout and did our best to continue. But we had not gone 50 yards before it became apparent it was impossible to go on. The ex-sergeant would just have to get up and walk. So he got up and walked; normally, painlessly, with no further complaints. The fraud had been exposed — but only after he had squandered our strength in a tremendous wasted effort to accommodate his demands!

The next day at camp, our ex-sergeant walked around normally, taking every opportunity to respond magnanimously to the remarks of the boys, some of whom he did not realize were poking fun at him. I was one of the guilty ones, still seething that such an apparently grown man could have so exploited us. It was a battle of the "self-centereds."

At the last camp-wide campfire of the week, all of the boys in my hike party who had volunteered to hike out and bring in the stretcher were recognized by being elected to the "Order of the Silver Marmot," a special Scouting inner circle to which most boys coveted entry. Usually it was reserved for older boys: Star, Life and Eagle Scouts who had distinguished themselves over several years of Scouting. In our case, the hike leader clearly wanted recognition for the boys who had proven themselves by actual service. They had come forward in his time of real need for support and included second class and first class Scouts. I was unrecognized, with only my conviction that I had been proven "right" to sustain me.

But I was left with a lasting lesson that becomes deeper and richer with time, together with other lessons that God has given me to help me understand clearly. I have learned painfully that God does not require my agreement with authority in order for that authority to warrant my support; nor does one have to be "deserving" in order to warrant my mercy and service. I have learned that being willingly defrauded is a necessity in order to be conformed into the image of Jesus Christ, who gave Himself up for me gladly and voluntarily that I might experience His salvation and righteousness in my life. He was defrauded of His life, but gave it willingly as it was extorted by the governing authorities, "not knowing what they were doing" and in violation of their own laws, putting their Creator to death. The Lord has used this in my life to illustrate the contrast between His nature and mine and to illustrate His true, life-giving principles of giving.

In addition, this experience and the exposure of my own sinful nature has been of great help in discerning and understanding the motives and attitudes of boys as they strive for recognition but frequently remain trapped in their own attitudes toward authority or the requirements of justice.

3

Taking Lessons from a Scout

"Thus the last shall be first, and the first last."
Matthew 20:16

Shortly after my marriage in 1961, my wife and I began to attend a Methodist church in Belmont, Massachusetts. One day I noticed in the church bulletin that the church sponsored a Boy Scout troop and I decided to become active again in Scouting. It had been nearly nine years since I had left Scouting behind in high school, but it seemed like a simple enough thing to show up at the troop meeting, only a few blocks from where I lived, and volunteer my services. What a shock it was for the Scoutmaster, Emil Wieher! But nearly every Scoutmaster, if he stays at it long enough, will reap the rare blessing of a "walk-on"!

It was not long before I was in harness, helping during the troop meetings and going along on the campouts, trying to teach all the things I already knew and totally oblivious to the fact that I was a learner, too. I recall that two of my earlier tasks were to teach knot tying and signaling Morse Code.

It became immediately apparent to me that one of the young boys in the troop, whom I will call "John," was much slower than the others. I concluded that he was mentally retarded and became acutely frustrated in my inability to teach him even the simplest things, no matter how hard I tried. In the knot tying, I finally retreated from all the basic knots and focused only upon Scouting's most basic knot, the square knot. I went over and over it with him for weeks, resolving that I would at least succeed in teaching him something fundamental. But at each meeting, I found that he had invariably forgotten everything from the preceding week. I concluded that he was retarded, unable to retain even the simplest skills, and not warranting such an inordinate portion of my time, while other boys were being held up in their advancement as a result. After two or three months of this, I resolved that a better strategy was to teach the other boys and to let John participate on an observational basis without forcing him to participate at a level where the pressure on him would be too great or where he would be embarrassed by exposure of his failures in having learned anything.

About this time, I commenced a troop-wide effort to learn Morse Code. The technique I used to teach was primarily through the use of 3x5 flash cards, upon which I had the Morse Code signal on one side and the correct letter of the alphabet on the other. I would teach letters according to the different groups by which their basic composition can be characterized; all "dits," all "dahs," symmetrical, asymmetrical pairs, etc., and finally finishing with the odd characters that fit no particular pattern. Using this method I could generally teach a group of boys the entire Morse Code within a couple of evenings, to a level where they were ready to send and receive flashing light messages. But as a test to ascertain that each boy had learned the code to a sufficient degree, I would have him go through the entire alphabet in front of all the other boys, the cards having been mixed at random.

One particular evening, we were reviewing each boy's readiness with the flash cards. There were about ten or twelve boys sitting in a circle and I had each boy whom I considered "ready" test his recognition level of the entire deck of cards. Generally, out of 26 characters in the alphabet, passing more than 22 was considered "good." Most of the boys were exceeding 20 on their first try. After I had completed testing each boy that I considered ready, someone asked,"What about John?"

I was embarrassed, because I had not planned to test John. I think I also felt uncomfortable with the fact that my bias had been revealed. Someone had exposed my double standard and now I was going to have to expose John to the ridicule of his fellow Scouts.

But I was trapped, so I asked, "Okay, John, do you want to try it?" "Sure," he said. So we proceeded through the flash cards. To my amazement, he missed only eight letters in the entire alphabet! I was relieved that he had not been embarrassed in front of the other boys, but I was also astonished. I had been sharply incorrect in my perceptions of John's ability to learn.

What was it that I was not understanding about John? How could someone whom I had written off have learned most of the Morse Code by merely watching? It was clear that there was more to John than I had first estimated.

A shocking discovery I made about Troop 234 was that none of them had ever been hiking. Even the Scoutmaster's son, who was an Eagle Scout, had never had a pack on his back! All of our campouts involved driving to the campground and carrying the gear from the car to the cabin or tent sites, only a few hundred yards. I developed a strong desire to lead the Scouts into the joys of backpacking I had experienced as a Scout.

With the Scoutmaster's approval, we undertook to buy Army surplus packboards and rucksacks and had several work sessions whereby we outfitted every interested boy with a very inexpensive packframe at least one level of quality better than I had enjoyed as a Scout, and we prepared for our first troop hike in August of 1963. In utter naiveté, I selected a route in the White Mountains of New Hampshire which far exceeded our capacities.

In typical Western disdain for the "Eastern molehills" which I thought were improperly called "mountains," I decided to take the troop from Franconia Notch, up over 3000 vertical feet to the summit of Mt. Lafayette, the last 1000 feet of which is above timberline, and to continue about three or four miles further along the ridge to the shelter at Mt. Garfield, where we would spend the night. In my inexperience in planning such trips, I also failed to get timely commitments from many of the boys and only about five showed up. This shortfall may have ensured our survival.

I had not carried a pack on my back for ten years. The other adult, a naval officer friend, Jack Richardson, had never even been hiking previously. It was the first time for all the boys. Also, lacking any experience in understanding the severity of the weather in the White Mountains, I did not comprehend the meaning of the winds and grey clouds over the mountains when we started out. But by the time we passed timberline, I began to realize we may have bitten off more than we could chew. The winds were blowing so fiercely that we were frequently blown off our feet. I estimated the wind to be 70 to 80 miles per hour. As we approached the summit of Mt. Lafayette, we struggled to maintain our equilibrium, leaning over at extreme angles and holding onto the boys' hands to keep them upright.

My ability to stand upright was helped somewhat by the secret 15 pound watermelon I was carrying in my pack, while periodically telling the boys that I understood that watermelons grew wild up on this particular ridge. But I paid a dear price lugging it to the top of Mt. Lafayette. By the time we reached the summit, we were all exhausted. We still had miles to go!

What an incessantly long ordeal it was, creeping slowly along the ridge toward Mt. Garfield. The trails in many places in the White Mountains are really only foot paths that follow the route of least resistance through the rocks and ledges. There has been no blasting, leveling or grading to speak of. Each step of that ridge seemed excruciating, up ledges, down ledges, over rocks, over roots...And the day just seemed to melt away on us while the weather got darker and more ferocious. Would we ever get to Garfield Shelter? Periodic raindrops hinted that things were about to get much worse. As nightfall approached, I began to reach a point of desperation not unlike my first Scout hiking ordeal, thinking that we had somehow passed the shelter! But no, there it was at last! A closed cabin with complete protection against the storm. We all went inside and collapsed.

There we were; a seven-person party and dinner had to be put together and served. Now I was the hike leader. I had to do the job and it was clearly going to be done alone. Jack lay on the floor of the shelter spread-eagled, face down, and did not move for nearly an hour. I went outside and began to cut wood and build a fire, putting the cooking pots on and boiling water. Soon one of the boys came out and asked what he could do to help. It was John. Without request and in the face of fatigue that must have been as great for him as for the rest of us, he was volunteering to help.

I was so tired and grateful for the help, I did not really comprehend what was happening. But I managed to "find" the watermelon out in the woods, sliced it up and served it. The rain began coming down in wind-driven sheets. John and I stood over the fire in our ponchos protecting the fire, preparing hot soup, some kind of stew and plenty of hot chocolate. No one else even put his head out the door. We served dinner and, without a word, John helped me to wash all the dishes and put everything away while the storms of hades raged outside. We went to bed while the roar of wind and rain pounded down upon the roof throughout the night.

In the midst of meditating on what our consequences would have been had we failed to reach the shelter and wondering about our next day's prospects, I realized without a doubt that I had totally misjudged John. This 12 or 13 year-old boy had all the character qualities of a complete man, and I thought that not many men would have been as gracious and uncomplaining as he had been in helping the party through this ordeal.

The next day it had stopped raining and we made it out on our exit route without any further difficulties. I went home thoroughly chastened in nearly all of my attitudes: toward the eastern mountains, toward my need for better planning, and toward my overly hasty judgment of boys. I learned a tremendous number of lessons on this first major trip which I led as a Scouter.

Yet there was another major surprise in store for me. I had not begun to measure the breadth of John! A few months later, we had a Scouting affair which required a special activity on a Saturday afternoon. John said he couldn't come, but didn't say why.

When I chanced to talk to his parents on the phone shortly thereafter, I discovered that the reason John had been unable to participate in that affair was that it had fallen on his regular Saturday for doing volunteer work at the hospital!

It is hard to fully express the powerful effect this had on the exposure of my own false standards and ideas I had of myself, for up to that point I thought that John was merely measuring up as a youngster to standards that I could also meet. But this placed things in an entirely different perspective.

John's actions and this new revelation of his life-style humbled me and helped me to see. Of what use is a square knot in living life? John was far down the road ahead of me, illustrating life principles that were so grand they placed my criteria of learning and skill development in shadow. I saw myself by comparison and knew I did not meet John's standards. Thereafter I had much greater tolerance in my judgments and attitudes toward boys.

I suppose also that John placed part of his life message into my life. He provided a standard for my own performance in working with boys under adversity for many years to come. He conditioned me to recognize that there is a higher value system, based on absolutes established by God rather than my own or other men's ideas. By sensing a Power that was beyond me working in the life of a mere youth, I may have also been sensitized to the later recognition of the truth of the gospel of Jesus Christ.

John's life has spoken many times over into the lives of other Scouts.

Scout Igloo Building

Igloo Village

4

Scoutmaster's Luck

"Blessed be the God and Father of our Lord Jesus Christ, who has blessed us with every spiritual blessing in the heavenly places in Christ, just as He chose us in Him before the foundation of the world..."

Ephesians 1:3-4

August of 1968 was the wettest August recorded in the history of the Pacific Northwest, and the third week turned out to be the wettest week of that month. I had scheduled the High Adventure Trip of Scout Troop 348 of Lake Forest Park, Washington for a traverse of the Alpine Lakes region lying between Stevens Pass and Snoqualmie Pass. I had planned to take the boys over a route which had not been previously traversed and which frequently had no trail. Almost the entire route is at or above timberline.

Washingtonians are used to their summer being dry. The occasional rain storms that blow in off the Pacific Ocean are usually gone in two or three days. Although the weather pattern we had been observing since the beginning of the month was clearly out of the ordinary, I clung to the hope that "any day now" the weather would clear and we would enjoy a spectacular trip. On the 17th of the month, off we started in the pouring rain!

Our route took us off the U.S. Forest Service road leading into Trout Lake at the north end of the planned route and we took the trail into Big Heart Lake, then cross-country via fisherman's trail to Chetwood Lake. Here began our true cross-country route finding. We had a number of "layover" days for the boys to fish and rest, but on these days I was obliged to go out with one of the other adult leaders and do the route finding for the next day. On each occasion, I would earnestly hope that the next day would clear up, figuring that the incessant rain could not continue forever, since it was contrary to the normal traditions of Washington's late summer weather.

But the rain continued. We enjoyed some benefit from being so high, generally from 5000 to 6000 feet in elevation the whole time, at which height the rain was usually more of a mist. On the other hand, our campsites were rather exposed and it put a premium on the Scouts' learning how to pitch their rain flies, build their fires and properly cook their food under somewhat adverse conditions. They did a super job of it and kept fairly dry. We heard few complaints — they were taking all of the rain in good style!

As the trip continued, we made our way to Williams Lake, over Dutch Miller Gap and south to Spectacle Lake, which at that time was also at the end of existing trail. From there it was cross country again for nearly the balance of the trip. On our layover day at Spectacle Lake, I ascended to the top of the ridge with my assistant Bill Schoening and one of the older boys, Will Deisher. We found a fantastic route to the top and climbed higher to spy out the rest of the next day's route over Alta Ridge, which would lead south to Rampart Ridge and our exit trail. The weather was miserable and seemed to be getting worse!

We built a small fire high on the ridge and ate some lunch while waiting for some kind of break in the clouds. I was discouraged by our failure to get good weather and now it was more important than ever because of the nature of Alta Ridge. It is a high, barren ridge which is quite rugged and requires quite exacting route-finding in order to avoid getting "hung up" in some impassable rock areas. Also, with the weather getting worse, I had a responsibility to use good judgment in not exposing the Scouts to weather or conditions which exceeded their capabilities. Eventually, the clouds did break and gave us a good view of the ridge we had to cross. We agreed our chances of making it were marginal in the type of weather we were facing.

The next morning we arose to more rain and clouds. As we ascended the ridge, it seemed to get worse. We continued to the vicinity of Park Lakes, where we had to make a decision one way or the other as to whether to attempt the ridge. As if in answer to our need for definitive direction, the heavens opened up and the rain poured down with more volume and fury than at any previous time in the trip. It clinched our decision. We would have to "bail out" and take our alternative "escape" route. It would require us to descend Mineral Creek to Kachess Lake a fair distance, but over trail which, according to maps, appeared to be only 10 or so miles to the end of a road. If we could get to the road before the end of the day, I would presumably be able to reach a phone with which to redirect our transportation arrangements to our alternative pick-up site.

Things did not go well at all. When we reached the outlet of Park Lakes, leading down into Mineral Creek, we found only old blazes on the trees and almost no trace of a trail. As we followed this down the hill, we found that what trail there was had not been maintained for many years. It had extensive fallen trees and debris around or over which we had to detour, slowing us considerably while we continued to absorb rainwater. As we reached the lower subalpine meadows, filled with lush waist-high plants and flowers, the vegetation was drooped over to such an extent that the trail was invisible. We followed it by shuffling along and "feeling" the trail with our feet while the plants poured their water into our clothes. The lower in elevation we went, the harder came the rain!

By mid-afternoon our misery began to reach new highs! We were totally drenched from the waist down. During rest stops we took off our boots and wrung out our socks. Our fingers and hands looked as if we had been washing dishes for weeks! But this was not my major concern. The day was wearing rapidly away, despite our best efforts to keep up the pace. The prospects for setting up a good camp in such a storm and after such an ordeal began to be a serious concern. We had to reach the end of the road and somehow find a way to the nearest telephone, which might be miles away at the nearest ranger station and would require my walking to get to it. But we also had to find a secure campsite, prepare a warm meal and get these boys into their sleeping bags.

We finally reached the northern end of Kachess Lake as it began to grow dark. Now, surely, we all thought, we would have good level trail the rest of the way. But this was not the case at all. The side of the lake was interrupted by a series of rugged ridges of rock over which the trail went first up, then down; up and down, interminably for nearly four miles. Our leg muscles for climbing would cool off and tighten up while descending and then be commanded to start up again and climb the next hill. Over and over this cycle was repeated in frustrating sequence, while it got dark and we began to hike by flashlight. All the while the rain just kept coming down harder and harder.

The Scouts' legs began to get rubbery. Boys began to trip and stumble as I called more frequent rest stops and warned them repeatedly to be careful of their steps. It was clear that we were on a precarious trail with frequent places where a bad stumble could result in a boy taking a trip all the way down into the lake! There was no place to stop and camp. But in the far distance, I began to think I could discern the hum of an engine. It was hard to tell in the roar of the rain and the slosh of the mud and I wondered where such a noise could be coming from, since we were so far from any civilization.

By 9:00 p.m. we were just hanging on and doing our best to avoid accidents. We were resolved to reach the end of the road safely and go to bed without supper if that was the price we would have to pay. In the meantime, we had all agreed that there definitely was an engine in the distance. About this time we caught sight of a single white light far off in the dark.

The end was in sight! We cautioned everyone and took even greater care in assuring that everyone reach it safely, stationing smaller boys between older, stronger ones or men. Then, as we approached within a few hundred feet of the light, we came to our last obstacle.

The end of the road had been geographically determined by a formidable stream which blocked its further construction without building a large bridge. Now we faced this stream and there was no footbridge! It was swollen to the very top of its banks by days of rain and today's downpour. The only way across was over a series of bare, slippery logs. While crossing, the boy in front of me slipped and fell in!

I grabbed his hand before he disappeared in the rushing water and held him until the boy in front could grab his other hand. Then we desperately tried to lift him up back up onto the log. Try as we might, while still carrying our packs, we could not lift the boy and his pack from the water. The stream pulled at him, threatening to tear him from our grasp and sweep him down into the lake. We were exhausted. What we might have been able to do if fresh, or on solid footing on a nice sunny day, was now beyond us. I told the boy we would have to try to lift his pack up enough for him to get his arms out and we would let the pack go! In the meantime, he seemed to slip more and more from our grasp as we struggled to hold on. At about the point where the water reached his rib cage, he shouted that his foot had hit some rocks in the stream bottom! Carefully, he placed part of his weight onto his foot while we renewed our grip and rested. Then we cautiously held him as he walked the rest of the raging stream, one step at a time, to the far bank. I was grateful when the entire party reached it without further mishap.

Like drowned rats, at 9:30 p.m. we trudged the last few steps up from the stream toward the white light. It was an electric light being driven by a gasoline generator. That was the explanation of the engine! Who could have brought a generator out to such a remote place? As we drew closer, we realized the light was under an open picnic pavilion and that the pavilion was filled with people — people with tremendous amounts of food! They saw us emerging from the darkness and turned to greet us. They were a group from the Boeing Outing Club, having one of their wilderness-style picnics. They were just finishing serving some several dozen of their group and had tables covered with uneaten hot food, desserts, hot chocolate and coffee. Would we like some? "Just have your boys put their packs over here under these rain flies and get in the chow line. We have paper plates, utensils; everything you need. Eat as much as you want!"

Stupefied by such a stroke of luck, we wasted no time eating as much as we could while I made arrangements with the leader to drive me to the nearest ranger station. Several huge canvas rain flies had been pitched and one of them was totally unused. It had more than the needed amount of room under it for us to lay out our ground tarps and sleeping bags.

By the time I got back from the ranger station everyone was fast asleep.

Scoutmaster's Luck 19

Cooking on Charcoal Stoves

Eating Coconut Cream Pie

What to Do in the Rain!

Wilderness Freedom — Chetwood Lake and Alpine Lakes High Adventure Trip — 1968

Ramblin' in Appalachian High Country Mt. Rogers/Mt. Mitchell High Adventure — 1979

5

Tasting Some Fruit

"Therefore, strengthen the hands that are weak and the knees that are feeble..."
                                                              Hebrews 12:12

In 1970, I planned another nine-day High Adventure Trip with my Scout troop to repeat the Alpine Lakes traverse of 1968 in the reverse direction. The section we had been obliged to bypass in 1968 due to rain was placed first, in hopes of getting over the high ridge connecting Alta Mountain and Three Queens Peak early in the trip with enough contingency time to allow for some weather delay. Wouldn't you know that we started out again (on July 25, the height of the dry season) in pouring down rain!

This was a new troop (Troop 530) from Port Orchard, Washington, and it was their first High Adventure Trip. It took us four slow hours, lugging heavy packs, to reach the end of the trail at Lake Lillian, where we commenced cross-country "bushwacking" through the waist-high azaleas, mountain ash and blueberries along Rampart Ridge. The bushes were soaking wet and soon we were, too. My thought was, "Oh no, not another trip like the one we had two years ago! Please, God, won't You stop the rain?" It continued to pour and we stopped, short of our original objective, at two beautiful mountain tarns where we set up camp. It continued to pour the rest of the evening and into the next morning. The next day's travel was the crux, the most difficult part of the traverse, so I decided to use one of our precious layover days to give the rain a chance to stop before we continued on. We lay in our tents playing cards. It rained all day and into the second night.

The third morning it was still raining, and we were enveloped in thick clouds, indicating some possibility of the weather breaking. Visibility was only about 100 feet. Reluctantly, I decided that we needed to go on, regardless, or else face the prospect of sitting here on the ridge for the whole nine days! We packed up our wet gear and pushed on.

The ridge was gentle and beautiful as we worked our way north across mostly open alpine meadows that had seen little travel. We soon came to Rampart Lakes and a short section in that vicinity that was heavily used by trail hikers. But by early afternoon we had reached Lila Lake, at the base of

Alta Mountain, our last sure landmark for some time to come. There we left all trails behind. Visibility had shrunk to about 50 feet and the weather seemed to be getting worse. I got out a compass and began to contour the side of the ridge to the point that I estimated from map study to be the place we would have to ascend straight up the side of the ridge. Starting up at the proper point was important because the contour maps showed steep cliffs at every point other than the route we were attempting to follow. By avoiding any stops over the last mile and traveling at a slow, steady pace, I hoped to minimize error in estimating distance traveled.

Finally, still traveling by compass and wristwatch, I announced we had reached the point where we would start up the side of the ridge. We had ascended only a few score feet when I recognized the trace of an old overgrown trail. I turned onto it, sensing that perhaps in years past, prospectors in this area might have constructed an access trail over this mountain. Sure enough, in a short while the trail switched back in the other direction, still ascending, then switched back again, and again, right up the side of the mountain and directly over the very summit of East Alta Mountain, the exact navigation point we were seeking!

But our joy was short-lived. We were high on the mountain and the weather began to deteriorate. The mist turned to heavy rain as we slowly descended down the north side of the mountain and traversed across steep hillsides on the ridge above Park Lakes. Down-sloping mountain ash and azaleas made the footing treacherous and we began to slip and fall frequently. To save distance, we decided against descending 1000 feet to the lakes to climb all the way back up again on the other side and so continued our "side-hill" route. Progress was painfully slow. By 7:30 p.m. we were only halfway across the slope! About that time a boy took a serious spill and broke his pack straps!

Oh, the joys of sitting in the pouring down rain with wet and demoralized boys, miles from the nearest trail, pulling out your pliers and repair kit, hoping that the carefully selected and rationed items therein will be suitable for repairing a pack carrying 50 lbs. of load! There was not more than another hour of daylight left in the day and we were stuck here, light-years from any emergency campsite, until I could fix the pack. Thirty minutes of work with grommets, split rivets and washers did the trick and we were on our way. But now it was evident we would be overtaken by dark while still stuck on the hillside in the rain.

I knew how the boys were taking all this. Their only hope was in finding a warm, dry place to sleep and receiving a good meal before going to bed. Now it was all slipping away. What could I do to alleviate their sufferings? I resolved that I would cook dinner for the whole group whenever we succeeded in finding a campsite.

Nine o'clock came and went and we were still forcing our way across the hillside when the slope began to ease somewhat and a few trees appeared. We were only about 30 minutes now from the high pass separating Park Lakes from Spectacle Lakes. The way became easier and the route to the pass lay entirely in sight. I told the other adult to follow the light of my flashlight, took one of the older boys with me and went ahead to build a fire in the pass where we would camp.

Simple joys take on prodigious qualities at the end of a bone-weary day when your hands are water soaked and your anxieties have been stretched for so long. The pleasure of reaching flat ground, taking off that pack, grabbing some firewood, striking the flame and seeing the warm blaze leap upward into the sky defies description. It served as a beacon to the boys on the slope and gave notice that a pleasant ending was at hand. By the time they trudged into camp there were two pots of soup boiling, ready to serve!

The rest was straightforward. After soup, the boys set up the tents while a sumptuous feast of rice, chicken and gravy was prepared and served to them, complete with lots of hot chocolate. The adults washed the dishes while the boys crawled into their sleeping bags and embraced a night's sleep that makes ordinary sleep pale by comparison.

The next day dawned — still cloudy but without any rain! We used another layover day to go exploring, traveling the high country to reach Glacier Lake, snow fields and climb Chikamin Peak, from which all the surrounding mountains could be viewed as from the top of the world! The weather gradually improved.

Now the trip began to take on overtones of victory. Another night's rain was scarcely noticed by the boys. Moving camp to nearby Spectacle Lake and cutting ample firewood for more heavy weather was routine. We began to catch fish. The Scouts were turning into veterans!

On the afternoon of the fifth day, the weather finally cleared. We were treated to bright skies and point-blank views of spectacular mountains, crystal clear mountain tarns, route finding over untraveled mountain meadows, climbs of high peaks, sliding down snowfields (and snowball fights in August!), exploring mining areas and fishing. What fun to fish in water so clear you could actually see the trout make their run at your spinning lure and strike at it before you felt the tug on your pole telling you he was hooked!

You could see the Scouts grow over the trip; cooperation, self-confidence, group cooking and camping skills were demonstrated routinely — young men who knew they had overcome the worst the wilderness could give them were now experiencing true "freedom of the hills."

Then came the last day down the trail; Scouts singing songs, whistling and shouting the jokes and special puns that have become part of the lore of this trip, a pace that will kill the adults if they don't deliberately slow the boys down occasionally, laughter and comradeship that envelops young men knowing they have accomplished something worthwhile.

Memories like these never fade from a boy's memory. They recall them often, especially in the spring when thoughts turn to the outdoors. Recollections fly to the tongue whenever old acquaintances are renewed. The memories of adventure and accomplishment are a form of treasure between young men. It enriches their relationship and aspirations for the future. The things they have accomplished become a standard, inspiration they will want to share with their sons.

Adventure gives life to boys.

Tasting Some Fruit 25

**Tasting the Fruit — Alpine Lakes,
Washington High Adventure — 1970**

**Cascade Crest Trail and Glacier Peak,
Cascade Mountains, Washington High Adventure — 1986**

6

Fixing Bill's Teeth

"For we are His workmanship, created in Christ Jesus for good works, which God prepared beforehand, that we should walk in them."
                                                                Ephesians 2:10

When the Navy transferred me to Bremerton, Washington, in 1968, I became active in Port Orchard Scout Troop 530 just as the Scoutmaster was leaving and so relieved him as Scoutmaster. One of the Scouts I inherited was a fantastic boy named Bill.

Bill was the most natural boy leader I have ever known. He was the Senior Patrol Leader, had just made Eagle Scout, and had a flair for organization and managing boys far beyond his years and Scout training. He seemed effortlessly to sense developing situations and to anticipate needed action. He never lost his temper, even in types of trying situations which frustrate most people. He was natural, unaffected and gifted in leadership. Here was a young man with unlimited potential for a productive future.

There was however, a problem with Bill not of his own making. His upper front teeth stuck straight out. I mean, they stuck out horizontally! It was not possible for him to close his lips over his teeth without special effort. The effect when I first met him was that my stomach turned; even as time passed I could not get my mind off the horrible distraction his teeth created from his wonderful personality and leadership qualities. I wondered how his teeth might affect his future and hoped that with more time I would get used to it.

It only took a brief inquiry to find out why his parents had never done anything about it. Bill's mother had been divorced and left with no job skills whatsoever. She was on welfare, trying to complete secretarial schooling to obtain work. She could barely put food on the table. Bill was a miracle boy of a hardship background. For some reason the idea of fixing his teeth as a project for the troop did not occur right away. But the problem continued to churn within me for nearly two years. Then something happened which helped me toward a solution.

In January 1970 (a day before the Navy informed me I was to be transferred to Vietnam later in the year) I shattered my knee playing basketball. It was my introduction to a period of severe pain and mental anguish during which a doctor attempted unsuccessfully to passivate my leg in a cast for five weeks. He had no success either in reducing the pain or in unlocking the broken cartilage in the knee. In desperation, I was ready to go to civilian doctors to get an operation when another Navy doctor looked with consternation on what the first had done and immediately made arrangements for me to have knee surgery.

The period following the surgery was extraordinary. I had never before appreciated the fact that people existed capable of such unselfish service as the young Navy corpsmen and nurses who waited on me and the other patients. I was totally dependent upon them for three or four days and observed with wonder the tireless efforts of 18 to 20-year old boys caring for a variety of sick and helpless patients with what appeared to be unconditional availability and commitment. It was a marvel to me. When I was released from the hospital, filled with gratitude and prospects of restored health, I was a transformed person — for a while.

I seemed to have a supernatural creativity and love in me I had never experienced before. It seemed to come from a Source apart from me and was so powerful I could actually feel its presence. It was wonderful. There were times I would just sit in gratitude and fellowship with this wonderful Spirit, not knowing where it came from or how to retain it. Before it slipped away several weeks later, I became motivated to do something about Bill's teeth.

It was immediately evident that Bill's mother would have nothing to do with an individual offering to pay for orthodontist work. I discussed with the troop committee the idea of the troop putting up the money through the contributions of willing men on the committee. One member put me in contact with an orthodontist who knew Bill's family and knew of his problem. I consulted with him and he confirmed that he knew Bill and that his teeth could be corrected with proper orthodontistry. He further offered to provide the services at cost, estimating that the whole job could be done for less than $1000.

Further discussions with the troop committee quickly resolved the financing. But the big problem was how to convince Bill's mother that this was something she wanted to let us do. She was a proud and upright woman, eager to earn her own way and not likely to accept such a gift in an area that she perhaps already viewed as "nonessential." I made an appointment to see her while still pondering the various approaches I could use. The more I thought about it, the closer to an idea I seemed to come. The day before I was to see her I suddenly came upon reasoning I knew she would be unable to refute. It was not only credible, it was the truth.

Bill's mother already knew generally what we wanted to do when we sat down to talk. She had her sales resistance up and made it clear at the outset that she was not accepting charity. Then I made my appeal to her.

"Mrs. M., we would like to do this for *selfish reasons*. It would make us feel good about ourselves to be able to do something worthwhile in your son's life. We admire him and feel that he has a promising future ahead of him. We would appreciate the opportunity to do something good in his life to help his success and happiness. We would be the ones getting the major benefit. We would be very grateful to you if you would let us do it, please."

She was totally disarmed. The issue she now had to resolve was whether or not she would stand in the way of our satisfying our own pleasure. It took only a moment for her to agree. The orthodontist work started right away, but I was transferred shortly thereafter and the work was still uncompleted.

Several years later I had the opportunity to get together again with Bill. We spent a beautiful late spring day out on a climb of one of the mountain peaks east of Seattle, fellowshipping in the challenge of the mountains. The orthodontist had done a beautiful job.

But we hardly talked about it. It is hard to say why Bill did not bring it up, but I knew why I didn't. It was as though I had a guard placed over my tongue. I was swept by the same refreshing spirit of knowledge that I'd had previously when the plan was being put together. This was not my work. As much as I would like to have claimed credit, there was no misunderstanding. God had done it out of His love for Bill. And so, as if standing in the presence of awesome riches or marvelous craftsmanship that cannot be comprehended and to which discussion adds no value, I didn't talk about it. We just enjoyed our fellowship and the strenuous day of adventure in the mountains.

7

High Adventure — Eastern Style!

"...We went through fire and through water..."
Psalm 66:12

In 1971, the Navy transferred me from a year's duty in Vietnam to Washington, D.C. and I moved my family to Alexandria, Virginia. I soon registered as Assistant Scoutmaster with a Scout troop which met only a few blocks from home. In 1973 I became Scoutmaster and began to wonder how I could implement some of the long-term High Adventure Trips we had included in our Scouting programs out west. Being a little reluctant to bite off a full nine-day trip with no experienced adult help, but discovering that the public schools in Virginia took a full week off from school early during the month of April, I hatched the idea of putting together a six-day trip to the high mountains of West Virginia. By "high" I mean in the vicinity of 4000 ft. in elevation. We made plans to camp at Spruce Knob, the highest peak in the state at nearly 4900 feet, and to follow this with a five-day hiking and fishing trip in the Cranberry Backcountry.

Spring in the east is capricious. It is possible to have temperatures in the 80's one week and in the 30's the next. We had ample balmy days during March and the Washington, D.C. area was bedecked in garlands of flowering trees and bulbs broadcasting the clear arrival of spring when we departed for West Virginia on April 5, 1974. We arrived there to the accompaniment of an "Arctic Express," a severe and prolonged surge of cold weather that roared in with accompanying wind and snow. Again, I had underestimated the severity of weather in the eastern mountains and the effects of only a few thousand feet of altitude.

The storm's arrival in full came during the first night while we were camped on the summit of Spruce Knob. We got up in the morning with three inches of fresh snow on the ground, the tents well iced and about 30 mile-an-hour winds. In packing up, our fingers soon went numb and I began to wonder, as so frequently in the past, what kind of a character builder this trip would prove to be. It seemed that so many first-time High Adventure Trips had much more than their fair share of adversity. On this trip I had two close naval officer friends who were on their very first campout with the Boy Scouts. Lieutenant Commander Chuck Bartholomew ("Bart"), an accomplished Navy diver who later went on to become the head of the U.S. Navy Diving and Salvage Office, was a tough and good-natured fellow, eager to try this "stuff" of camping with the moral support of our close German naval officer friend, Commander Helmut Schmidt of the Federal Republic of Germany Navy, assigned to our Navy program office. They both kept a stiff upper lip and good humor as things proceeded to get worse.

Driving down to the Cranberry Backcountry, one of our automobiles broke down and had to be left by the side of the road while arrangements were made to have it towed to a garage and repaired. It was 15 degrees Fahrenheit and snowing when we finally started out on the Frosty Gap trail shortly after noon. All day it snowed while we trudged along the combinations of trail and logging roads to the Summit Lake Shelter. A good hot dinner served us well and gave us a better opportunity to observe some of the characteristics of young boys making the best of an ordeal.

Camping tends to magnify the fact that boys and men are not normally highly organized in the care and keeping of their personal things. Such things as clothing, dishes, food, hygienic gear, etc. are areas that "mother" has always taken care of and it would be totally out of character for young Scouts to suddenly take intense care in maintaining these things. It is normal for them, if left to their own devices, to leave underwear and socks strewn about on the ground, boots left open for the rain to fill, food bags unaccounted for and utensils scattered everywhere. Adversity doesn't change the situation; it only magnifies the effects.

If your boots are too cold and stiff to put on in the morning, then just walk around in them with your feet only half in them, on their sides. Or walk around in the dirt and mud in your brand new $8.00 per pair 100% wool socks. Pick up another boy's cup and use it if you can't find your own. "That's not my underwear left out on the ground" really means, "I wouldn't know my underwear, anyway. Besides, who cares? I don't plan to change mine for the whole week." The wise Scoutmaster will try to understand the tremendous cultural gap each young boy is trying to breach in his own development of organization, while assuring that mission-critical gear is kept as operational as possible so as not to jeopardize a successful trip. Each boy eventually comes around to a new measure of organization, good at least for short spurts of Scouting, until he returns to his mother's womb at the end of the trip. Sometimes mothers even notice a permanent difference!

On this trip, Mike, a boy who later went on to make Eagle Scout, was still a raw tenderfoot, full of enthusiasm, but still totally spontaneous and disorganized in his personal management. He required lots of help, and took it all good-naturedly. He seemed to enjoy the trip immensely, even though he was clearly the leader in wet socks, lost articles and difficulties in getting his frozen boots to fit!

The third day was clear and had warmed up to 25 degrees. We set our expectations on improved weather for the rest of the trip and hiked down several miles to the Cranberry River, where we set up our tents and rain flies for a two-day layover and some good fishing. The weather warmed a bit further and one of the boys caught a nice trout shortly after we set up camp. However, that day turned out to be our only respite. Rain and snow started again that evening and the layover day was miserable. Staying close enough to the fires to stay warm was a strenuous exercise in twisting and moving around to avoid the smoke that swirled wildly in the shifting winds. The most comfortable place to be was in our sleeping bags in the tents, playing cards. We concentrated on our meals and caught a grand total of only two trout in the Cranberry River.

The fifth day found us breaking camp to the sound of ice clattering off the tents while wind-driven snow continued to fall. We started up the U.S. Forest Service road, which made the walking easy despite an accumulation of about six inches of snow of the ground. The camp we made that evening was one of the most miserable of my life.

The only flat ground we were able to find which wasn't filled with trees and offered promise for tents was a nearby abandoned logging road. The frozen ground did not yield up its rocks easily and we were obliged to find places for our bodies to fit between them. Although there was plenty of firewood, even the standing snags had spent the entire winter in ice and snow and tended only to smoulder, requiring extraordinary measures of stacking the wood to dry above the fire before they would burn well. To assure that everyone had access to sufficient heat, we built a fire against the bank of the old road that was about 12 feet long and set a series of log benches in front. We continued to lay long logs in the fire while we cooked and dried clothing, but the smoke from the wet wood nearly overcame our eyes and noses! There was no avoiding it if one wanted to receive the heat of the fire!

This last campsite was the straw that broke the back of my two navy friends who had come along to find out more about this camping "stuff." Poor Helmut lay writhing amidst the rocks on the cold ground in his $150 down sleeping bag, on top of his $1.50 plastic air mattress which had gone flat the second day of the trip. With little insulation underneath, the cold and the rocks kept him awake all night, his trial broken only by his having to get up and relieve himself in the snow while barefooted! Nothing I could say to him in future years ever erased his memory of that night.

The last day dawned bright and beautiful. Only three miles remained to our cars up a road that in the space of a few hours began to shed its snow under the warm sun. Birds sang in the trees. The adjacent stream sounded merry and cheerful where only yesterday its voice had been swept away by the wind in the trees. It was spring all over again.

Mike was full of exuberance and eager to be the first one to finish. He stayed ahead of the troop as we walked up the road in twos and threes. I told Bart that he would break into a run as soon as he spied the cars and would probably trip in his eagerness to be first to the cars. As we came around the last bend in the road, I hollered to Mike as he was already beginning to break into a run, "Don't run, Mike! You'll fall flat on your face!" The words were hardly out of my mouth when, SPLAT! Mike tripped and his pack drove him face down into the mud and slush! So much for untimely warnings!

Later, Mike's mother told me how much he had enjoyed the trip, how he talked about nothing else at the dinner table for days thereafter, and was seen to put on his pack and hike around the neighborhood for the sheer fun of it several days later.

Ten years later, I was paying a bill at a local restaurant when a tall man with a beard greeted me from a few feet away, "Hi, Mr. Duff! Do you remember me?" I looked hard at him and began to think I might see some similarity between him and one or more Scouts I had had years earlier. Before I struggled too hard, he introduced himself by name and told me briefly what he was now doing and I did the same. It was only a matter of a minute or so before he brought up the memory of the "great West Virginia trip," which was one of his strongest and fondest recollections of his Scouting career.

But I never again got either of my two friends to go camping with me!

High Adventure — Eastern Style! 35

**Misery in West Virginia High Country
1974**

**Finishing the Rapids, Allagash River
Maine High Adventure — 1989**

8

Scouts Will be Boys

"Discipline your son while there is hope, and do not desire his death."
Proverbs 19:18

Scouts can be steel-willed and aggravating. Men who were once boys can be confounded when they confront familiar foolishness staring at them through the eyes of a young boy who is dead certain he has the universal answer to a problem. As the Scouter grows from one incident to another, he gradually accumulates some understanding of how to deal with each type of problem. He compiles a sort of reference inventory from which to deal and he discovers that some principles are more important than others; but God is uncanny in his ability to come up with new situations which give the Scoutleader whole new problems to try to solve. I think it is a bottomless well from which we go on drawing and learning as long as we live.

One common situation which has become much more severe with the recent growth in fast food eating habits is the Scout's limited taste for different foods. It goes far past the dislike of liver and onions or hominy grits which typified my boyhood. Now the boys turn up their noses at most kinds of soup, macaroni and cheese, hot cereals and other common and nourishing foods, mainly because they haven't grown accustomed to them and because their parents haven't resolved that they will eat what is served or won't eat at all. The boys have been given an upper hand, it seems, in dictating what is placed upon the family table, and so there is nearly always a confrontation of some sort when Scouts go on their first campout. A typical conversation goes something like this.

>   Scout: I don't like butterscotch pudding (or tomato soup, or cream-of-wheat...)
>   Scoutmaster: Have you tried any lately (or at all)?
>   Scout: No, but (I think) I did once when I was young and just know I don't like it.
>   Scoutmaster: Well, you'll have to try some on this trip, at least one serving.
>   Scout: I won't eat it. I don't like it.

My policy over the years has been to require all of the Scouts to eat some of everything on the menu, unless the boy is obviously ill or other problems supercede the importance of disciplined eating. Seldom has it proved to be a big issue once the Scout knows that the Scoutmaster means business.

And usually in a short period of time, the Scout has no problem with either the food or the policy.

On Steve's first campout, however, he had his first confrontation with pea soup. He sat there at the table following a conversation something like the above, and stared at his half cup of soup while it got cold. Periodically he was encouraged to go ahead and eat it before it got any colder (with the promise that once he had done so, he would receive the rest of his meal). He continued to rest his head on his hands, staring at the soup as it began to congeal on the top as it cooled. This went on for about 15 minutes and his soup became stone cold. He held on for quite awhile and the Scoutmaster's resolve began to waver when he observed Steve's skin begin to pale and break out into a cold sweat! He was actually making himself sick at the mere prospect of having to drink that soup!

I pointed out, "Steve, you're making yourself sick by imagining all sorts of things about that soup that aren't true. Go ahead and try some. You haven't even tasted it yet."

Steve sat there staring at the soup until his face became as white as a sheet. About that time the other Scouts, who had finished their soup and the main course as well, took a spice cake and a gingerbread cake out of our campfire oven. The aroma passed over the table, and I suppose Steve must have been getting some kind of persuasion from his stomach that this was all about to pass beyond his reach if he did not respond. Out of the corner of my eye, I noticed him dip the tip of his spoon into the cold soup, lift it to his tongue and taste it. He wrinkled his face and jerked his head back and forth in an awful grimace, conveying the suffering he was experiencing. In a few more moments he did so again, with even more glorious histrionics. Nobody paid any attention to him. Then he repeated the process a third time, and a fourth, and so on. His facial expressions and head jerks began to subside and before long he was dipping his spoon and bringing it to his mouth the way most people eat their soup. Soon it was all gone. He showed me his cup.

"Look, Mr. Duff, I finished it!"

"Well, you sure did. Nice going! Step over there and get some of the main course. Then you can have some cake."

In a year or two, Steve had pea soup on his list of favorites, telling me he asked for it to be served at home and placing it on some of our campout menus. The thought never occurred to me, however, in the face of the trauma that he had affected, that he would forget that he had ever disliked it.

Some years later, though, when Steve was nearing 20 years of age, I had a pleasant reunion visit with Steve and his family and brought up the pea soup incident. He stared at me with a blank face.

"What?" he exclaimed.

I recounted the story to him in more and more detail as it became evident that he did not recall the incident. He continued to protest that it was not possible that he had ever disliked pea soup!

One area of taste, however, to which the boys seem to become more and more impervious with time is canned sardines. We take them on High Adventure Trips for high protein/high fat lunch snacks on a menu where most of the food is dehydrated and it is hard to get much meat and oil into the diet. Twenty years ago kids had little trouble learning to like sardines. But it seems now that only by the last day of the trip is there enough of an adjustment to their craving for something from McDonalds' that they are willing to eat more than their mandatory one sardine! Only about 50% of the boys seem to really develop a taste for them. Tastes seem to be becoming more and more rigid and the sardine policy may have to come under serious reexamination soon!

One of the most frequent areas of vain warning given to Scouts is that too much heat from a campfire will ruin wet leather boots. There seems to be a streak of knowledge inside each boy by which he knows that the Scoutmaster doesn't have the whole picture. Each Scout knows that he can rest his booted feet near the fire without harming the leather of his boots. Despite eagle eyes and heroic efforts to save the investment of parents in their boys' footwear, there is always a regular stream of incidents in which boots have become brittle or burned through, sometimes with melted soles, as wise young outdoorsmen have sought to overturn laws of physics.

Rain also brings out a sadistic streak in the few boys who seem to have adopted for themselves the responsibility of keeping alive the grand old tradition (which seems to be coast-to-coast in the USA, at least) of cutting down tents. On one occasion we were well into the high mountains and had a heavy night of rain. I awoke to find that a particular boy had cut all the tents except his and the Scoutmaster's! I had anticipated trouble with him the previous day and warned the entire troop not to do that very thing. But he didn't listen and I had the job of finding appropriate discipline. I responded by having him carry out the two tents he had cut down and which had become totally water soaked. It was about 20 additional pounds which he had to carry out, approximately five miles. He collapsed about a mile from the end, and I carried them the rest of the way. I believe he learned his lesson.

Another Scout, Jim, was a particularly hard-headed boy and very rebellious; he had come from a broken home. However, there were other aspects of Jim's character which required time to emerge and for me to understand. One of them was his insecurity and fear, covered by bravado. This resulted in his suddenly having anxiety attacks, reaching fright levels to the point that he could not function; he could not even follow instructions which would solve the problem. On one spring trip, we took a day hike out of camp up one of the nearby peaks in the Cascade Mountains of Washington. Most of the slopes were still covered by late winter "corn snow," which provided a firm surface upon which to walk. As we ascended, the slope of the snow increased. Suddenly Jim froze, clawing the snow with his fingers and unable to move. I went to him and slowly talked him into a standing position. He was experiencing a severe case of mountaineering "exposure"; in this case, fear of slipping and falling down the snow slope. It is normal among all people at some degree of extremity, and usually can be overcome to ever-increasing degrees by instruction and experience. But Jim had reached his limit and another 15 minutes of instruction and encouragement produced no results. He was frightened to the point of tears. I had to take him back down the hill, but taking him all the way back to camp was out of the question without cancelling the day's objective for the whole troop. I got him to a large flat rock out in the sun and told him to stay there until we returned for him. He was not to attempt finding his way back to camp by himself! For the next several hours, while we were ascending the peak and returning, I worried about Jim. Would he obey? Or, having recovered his nerve, would he attempt to compensate for his poor showing by "proving" that he could find his own way back to camp?

As we came back down the mountain slopes, tobogganing down the snow on our plastic ponchos, I was glad to see that Jim had not moved. He had stayed right where I had told him to. As I approached to congratulate him, he did not even let me get the words out of my mouth.

"Look, Mr. Duff, I didn't move. I stayed right here, just like you told me." He had been reading my mind!

On another trip, a High Adventure, we had a four or five-mile uphill grade facing us one afternoon. I noticed that Jim didn't seem to care for the menu at lunch so I emphasized to the boys that they were not to pocket their food or candy, as they needed the energy to get up the hill. Jim didn't obey, giving most of his crackers and cheese away to other boys and pocketing his peanut brittle. I didn't discover this, however, until mid-afternoon when he collapsed in the trail, his face pale and all his strength gone. I recognized the symptoms and asked him what he had done with his lunch. He was quick to confess, and was impressed by the consequences. What a great teacher experience is! However, it took me an additional two hours to nurse him up the trail, carrying part of his load and helping him to recover some strength with hard candies. But the after-effects caused him to stay in his sleeping bag the next morning, a layover day, and to skip breakfast. He consequently missed our day hike, knowing he would finish the trip with only 49 total miles hiked, not enough for a Boy Scout 50-miler Award. So the consequences of his disobedience left a lasting impression on him. The next year he announced to me at the outset that he was going to take special care to eat all his food and go on all the day hikes. He was not going to miss out on another 50-miler Award!

It is not uncommon to have a Scout on his first campout suddenly develop the blank stare of homesickness, with tears and heart-rending pleas to be taken home. It usually occurs when the young Scout, not yet well bonded in fellowship with his patrol members, is left alone with no particular camping or hiking tasks to accomplish. His mind begins to wander to his mother and his bed at home. But it can sometimes be aggravated by the sudden discovery that he has drawn dishwashing chores, as well. I have seen it persist, also, in spoiled sons, and once experienced profane demands from a 14-year old Scout to be taken home, 75 miles away, following a thunderstorm in which his tent blew down. This was the same tearful boy whom I had hugged and comforted to sleep on his first campout three years previously. But this was a boy who had lost his father and received little or no discipline except that which he received through Scouting.

I could buy all the new tents I ever needed if I had a dollar for every Scout who has tripped over a tent guy line or ripped one out of the tent while running past the tents after he has been told both not to run in the campsite and to keep clear of the guy lines. There is also not a single spoon or spatula in our cook kits that lasts more than six months before the handle is burned by someone's leaving it in the pot or on the griddle while still cooking over the fire, despite repeated warnings not to leave a utensil on the fire. How many meals have been burned simply because the boys decided not to follow cooking rules and procedures that had been faithfully taught them! Boys are spontaneous and forgetful, wanting to wrestle, run, test and tease. The result of most of the things they do is eventually destructive, if not disciplined. Yet they also want to win approval and are inspired by vision. They can be led by someone willing to walk with them and share their experiences.

Love is a unique marriage of mercy and accountability. Boys need both. Accountability drives foolishness far from boys (Prov. 22:15), by giving them understanding that there are inescapable consequences for their actions, either right or wrong. Mercy pays the consequences of the boy's mistakes rather than requiring the boy to pay. Learning to minister these two gifts together works effectively also to drive foolishness far from the Scoutmaster. Boys will be boys. Nothing one can say or teach will cause their thoughts, behavior or attitudes to change overnight. The Scoutmaster inherits what is delivered to him in boy-shaped packages and they become his discipline. He must find answers to their problems that satisfy his own standards for "doing his best" to do his duty for God and his country and in obeying the Scout Law.

And they give him stories to last a lifetime.

9

Christmas Trees — 1973

"There is a way which seems right to a man, but its end is the way of death."
Proverbs 14:12

Some time after taking over as Scoutmaster of Troop 659 of Alexandria, Va., I became involved in an incident which caused me a great deal of pain and anger. I dealt with it in a manner which I thought right at the time, not realizing that I was laying seeds which would grow into a great root of bitterness. It was years before God brought the matter back before me with the requirement that it be straightened out.

What had happened was this. Our sponsoring church institution had a men's club which sold Christmas trees every year as a fund-raising project. One of the features of the arrangement with the two Scout troops which the church sponsored was that we would help with the sales and at the conclusion of the two or three-week effort, each troop would receive a check for the services rendered by the boys. This seemed an equitable arrangement and served also to provide some contact between the men of the church and the two Scout troops. Although the Scout hut was provided by the church as well, it was not very well maintained at the time, and we never had any contact or participation by the men of the church other than at the time of Christmas tree sales.

Following the Christmas tree sale of 1973, the Scoutmaster of the other troop, whose name was Bill and who was a member of the men's club, told me that the club was going to keep part of the money due the troops and use it to build a portable shed so we could get out of the weather while selling trees the next year. Since the function of the hut was solely to support the Christmas tree sales, and the costs had to be borne out of the men's club funds, it was their reasoning that the Scouts' fees should be reduced accordingly. The checks we normally received at that time were not large — of the order of $150 per Scout troop, so a sizeable reduction meant essentially that we had worked nearly for free and would have to seek other sources of funding to cover such essential things as troop supplies and annual registration fees.

I agreed with Bill in his concern and felt that it was unfair for the men's club to deduct what was essentially a capital investment decision from the stipend to the troops for their labor in support of the sales. I decided to appeal to the men's club and Bill made arrangements to place us on the next monthly meeting agenda for that purpose.

Bill kept me advised of events over the next month or so. During that period, I was not given a hearing with the men's club and a decision was finalized by them to give the troops significantly reduced checks. This heaped coals on my anger, by unfairly denying me an opportunity to appeal or state our point of view. What had previously been a situation of tolerable neglect between sponsor and Scout troops now became overt and intolerable. I felt I had been cheated and then scorned.

I was upset and angry. I wrote a letter to the men's club stating how I felt and breaking off the arrangements of Troop 659 to assist in future Christmas tree sales. It was appropriately indignant and articulate, I thought, leaving no doubt as to how I felt. I had Bill read the letter and then mailed it. There was no response.

Troop 659 went on to begin raising money through donut sales, paper drives and other typical Scout fund-raising efforts and I never really seriously looked back at the action I had taken. I had been prepared to seek another church sponsor for the troop if a further issue was made of the Christmas tree incident or if the troop reached a point of financial difficulty where we needed a closer relationship with a sponsor. But since no such issues were ever raised, we went our own way and the matter faded from memory.

A year later the Navy transferred me from Alexandria to Seattle, Washington. I did not know that events would transpire there which years later would make my letter to the men's club a burning issue.

10

Not an Eagle

"My people are destroyed for lack of knowledge..."
Hosea 4:6

One of a Scoutmaster's greatest joys is in seeing one of his Scouts culminate years of skill and character development by attaining the rank of Eagle Scout. This is the highest rank in Boy Scouting, and achieving it requires an unusual amount of dedication and accomplishment. It is a fairly rare occurrence; statistics range from about 1 in 50 to 1 in 200 of all boys who enter Scouting who actually attain the rank of Eagle.

The rank of Eagle Scout is recognized as equivalent to one year of college by the armed forces in selecting and assigning recruits. It is also recognized by colleges as one of the more significant reflections of accomplishment among male students applying for college admission.

One of the Scoutmaster's chief tasks — in fact, the very substance of his role with Scouts — is to help them formulate and obtain achievable goals. This involves discernment and encouragement of the boy's own objectives, quite often never previously vocalized, as well as challenging and leading Scouts to greater accomplishments than they will frequently set for themselves. It also requires working carefully so as not to exceed a Scout's capacity. Scouting has a graduated set of skills and leadership development opportunities which take into account the tremendous range of physical and emotional growth changes which occur in boys from ages 11 to 17, and the Scouting program has plenty of flexibility in which boys can grow at their own rates while continuing to make progress in discreet steps. Still, there are many "off-ramps" which cause boys to fail to pursue their goals or to drop out of Scouting, and many of these factors are beyond the Scoutmaster's control.

During my first 15 years as an adult Scouter, I was frequently transferred from one military duty station to another and, as a result, served with six different Scout troops during that period. One of the consequences was a tremendously long period in which I did not see any fruit of my efforts in the form of boys making Eagle Scout. As well as I can recall, I only witnessed two boys making Eagle Scout during that period, and I had significant investment and relationship with neither. I had almost no opportunity to continue relationships with the younger boys who shared in all the major learning adventures and it grieved me that I never even knew if any of them made Eagle, much less have the opportunity to participate in their accomplishment. By late 1977, as I faced the prospects of again leaving a Scout troop to which I was deeply attached, none of whom had yet made Eagle, this had become an oppressive issue and I began to pray that God would enable me to see the fruit of Eagle Scouts. I recall one day in which I travailed in quite a heavy spirit of prayer over the subject. Shortly after this I received an unexpected letter.

It was from a Midshipman at the U.S. Naval Academy. Somehow he had come across my name and been prompted to write me a letter. I was halfway through it before I realized it was from one of my former Scouts in Troop 530, Port Orchard, Washington. He went on to tell me of his father's subsequent changes in duty, his decision to go to the Naval Academy, and so on, and casually mentioned that he had made Eagle Scout before leaving Scouting. In his closing line he returned to this thought and wrote, "I just thought you'd like to know that one of your boys made Eagle Scout!"

This remarkable answer to prayer also gave me encouragement that in the future I would have more opportunity to witness growth in the boys I served. This indeed came to pass when, in 1978, I returned to Alexandria, Va. and was given the chance to serve a second time with Scout Troop 659 for 11 more years. Nearly all the Scouts were boys whom I had brought in as Scoutmaster three years or so earlier. Here I learned through experience the trials and difficulties in helping a boy to get to the rank of Eagle Scout all the way from Tenderfoot and of the importance of the right kind of assistance needed from the Scoutmaster for many boys to make it. I was confronted with a large number of Scouts who came extremely close to making Eagle but, for a wide variety of reasons not limited to cars and girls, didn't quite make it prior to their 18th birthday. Sometimes a single merit badge or an unfinished project is all that remains uncompleted. It is a mystery. Something akin to paralysis of the will sets in as a boy makes the transition into college or the work world. His vision changes and his will to carry through on the remaining few requirements weakens. Nearly every boy later regrets that he did not make that last bit of effort that would have been sufficient. But it cannot be undone. So the rewards have become doubly rich for those who succeed because of the many who fail, and in so doing illustrate the difficulty of achieving Eagle status. Each failure is one which grieves the Scoutmaster, causing self-examination and a review of lessons learned to help increase the next boy's chances of success.

One of my most useful lessons has been in realizing the inability of most boys to organize their time and priorities for planning new activities. I was surprised to discover that older Scouts, although extremely competent in their camping and leadership skills, have the same degree of disorganization in their planning of nonroutine activity as Tenderfoot Scouts do in the management of their personal camping gear! Identification of remaining merit badges, selection of order of work, identification of steps necessary to become qualified in the requirements, identification of resources (counselors, materials, booklets, etc.) and scheduling is extremely difficult because most older teenage boys do not understand the process just outlined. Hence, it frequently requires bringing the boy to the table and "loading his pencil" to get the particulars onto a piece of paper. Following this, it is only slightly less difficult to help the Scout organize his time to resist the unpredictable demands of school, band, sports, other extracurricular activities and the always present unexpected changes in circumstances which delay things. Generally, though, once a plan is on paper, it is a much more manageable affair and the primary problem shifts to finding a satisfactory means of accountability to monitor progress and track needed changes in the plan.

But not all problems are as easy to understand as cars, girls, changing visions or planning. The following story illustrates that there are other unfathomables sometimes too deep for a Scoutmaster to discern with confidence. Included in these are such questions as, "Where is the true blessing for the boy? What lessons does he have to learn? How do I give him the best opportunity to learn these lessons with a minimum amount of grief? When do I let go and trust God to build the character that I have been unable to build? How do I find and do what is right?"

A boy I will call Jeff was one of my best Scouts. For a number of years he had demonstrated superior performance in all his Scouting skills and leadership qualities. He had a delightful and open personality. He was effective in dealing both with adults and younger boys. As a Life Scout he served as Senior Patrol Leader and I considered him to be one of the two best Senior Patrol Leaders I had had in that Troop over a period of six or seven years. One spring day he told me he was getting a job which would prevent his coming to Scout meetings or campouts, but that he didn't want to drop out of Scouts. He was just in the process of getting his Eagle project approved, and I told him that becoming inactive in Scouts was incompatible with advancement to Eagle; he should seek to change his working arrangements or get a different job. A few weeks later he told me he had taken the job. His Eagle project plan completed its approvals at the same time.

Thus began a long odyssey, lasting a year and half, in which we saw very little of Jeff. Over that span of time he never went on another campout with the troop. Every few months, when we would figure we had seen him for the last time, he would drop in near the end of the troop meeting on his way home from work at the bank, dressed in his suit, to renew the dialogue.

Each time he would reassert that he considered himself to be an active Scout, still planning to make Eagle. The dialogue continued something like this over five or six occasions:

"Jeff, you must change your job hours and get active in the troop. I cannot recommend you for Eagle as an inactive Scout."

"I have a right to work. I want to earn money and get ready for college."

"Right! That is not the issue. You are free to work. But you must find some appropriate solution to both working and Scouting, if you choose both. You cannot have it both ways and expect to make Eagle Scout while having dropped out of the program. Participation is an essential factor in illustrating Scout Spirit and in maintaining active status in the troop."

"I'll take my chances."

During most of the next year and a half, Jeff made little effort on his Eagle project, and except for the principles involved, the issue appeared as though it would prove academic. But in the summer just prior to his eighteenth birthday, he began work in earnest and on the evening prior to his eighteenth birthday, he walked into the Scout meeting hut with a completed Eagle Scout application, including a certification of his having successfully completed his Eagle project! He handed it to me — and with it handed me a dilemma.

Here was a boy I liked and respected very much, who I wanted very much to attain Eagle. On the other hand, he had flouted reasonable authority and clearly articulated guidance regarding the conditions upon which I would give him a favorable recommendation for Eagle. On the other hand, should I adhere to this issue alone? What if I were wrong? What would I be trying to prove? What were the real issues associated with Jeff being given a favorable recommendation for Eagle Scout? I agonized over this for a week or so, praying, reviewing the assertions I would be making in the Scoutmaster signature block and seeking counsel from other men in the Scout district. Finally, I signed the Eagle application with an asterisk by my name and an explanatory letter stating that my approval was conditional on Jeff's providing an additional six months of satisfactory service to Scouting. In the letter I outlined three alternative approaches in which Jeff could satisfy this condition: 1) either as an Assistant Scoutmaster to some Scout troop in the vicinity of the college he would be attending, 2) as a member of Scouting's own service organization, Order of the Arrow, to which Jeff had already been initiated, or 3) through his college's Scouting service fraternity, Alpha Phi Omega.

I reasoned that by placing my recommendation in a form in which the

District Eagle Board of Review could consider it along with Jeff's credentials and attitudes, I would also be submitting to higher authority; that they would also have the opportunity to scrutinize my attitudes and position and overrule me if they thought me wrong.

My position brought me into immediate conflict with the District Eagle Advancement Chairman. He wanted me to give unconditional approval, inasmuch as the District could not forward to the national headquarters a "conditional" approval such as I had recommended, and there was no precedent for the District in resolving such an action. He also sympathized with the boy. In the end, it was decided the District would also leave it up to the Eagle Board of Review and, if my views were supported, the Eagle Application would be held by the local Council office pending Jeff's satisfaction of the six month service requirement. A special Council area member was added to the board to participate in the proceedings.

The week before the Eagle Board of Review I met with Jeff, explained to him the position I had taken and counselled with him how I thought he should deal with the board. I emphasized my opinion that if the Board members sensed that he recognized he had made a mistake in the course he had taken, they would override my recommendation and approve his Eagle rank without further qualification. I explained the power of admitting a mistake in dealing with a conflict such as this and left sincerely hoping that he believed this was true and would act accordingly.

The evening of the Eagle Board, I introduced Jeff to the members, explained the circumstances summarized in the letter and departed to keep a later appointment to brief our sponsoring church representatives on the past year's Scout activities. Near the conclusion of the evening, while I was packing up a slide projector and materials, Jeff walked through the open door of the church fellowship hall in which the church sponsors had met, shouted "NO!", and walked back out. Though I did not understand his meaning, I knew that things had not gone well.

I later found out that Jeff had taken a hard position with the Eagle Board of Review and maintained that he had been right in his actions; that Scouting had no right to expect any more of him as a condition for his Eagle rank. After a long and difficult discussion, the Board had voted unanimously to support my position. The basis of their action was that Jeff had not met the prerequisite for satisfactory "Scout Spirit."

During the following months, the District Eagle Advancement Chairman, having disagreed with me and the subsequent Eagle Board action, attempted to make alternative arrangements for Jeff. He promised Jeff that if he would come into town from his down-state college some time during the fall, he would set up another Eagle Board of Review for him and get the action of the first Board overturned. As the Eagle Advancement Chairman later explained it to me, he received only excuses from Jeff; "Well, it's a long bus ride." "If I come home on holidays, I'll be busy with other things." "I'm too busy studying." Then the Eagle Advancement Chairman concluded, "I guess you were right, after all. Jeff's heart was really not in it. He has no Scout Spirit."

And so a boy who seemed more deserving in many respects than many others who have attained their Eagle Scout award failed to earn his, despite the fact that there were many well-intentioned people working on his behalf. Did we make a mistake? Has the boy learned a more important lesson that will someday prove more valuable than an Eagle pinned on his breast? God only knows.

I think I did the right thing but still grieve and question every time I think about it.

11

I Shall Supply Your Needs

*"My God shall supply all your needs
according to His riches in glory in Christ Jesus."*

Philippians 4:19

In January of 1976 I received Jesus Christ as Lord and Savior. Dramatic signs and wonders followed and major changes took place in my life. In the months following, I found a church near our home in the Woodinville, Washington area and began attending with my family. During that spring, as the Navy ship testing program* I had been conducting in Southern California drew to a close, I prepared to seek out and again associate with a local Boy Scout Troop. In the 14 years and half-dozen or so troops in which I had been working in Scouting up to this time, I had never comprehended Jesus Christ or that God might undertake to bless boys through such a program. I was now growing rapidly in Him as He changed my life, but had yet to experience anything from God in the area of working with boys.

After returning full-time to the Seattle area with the Navy, I attended one or two troop meetings of a Scout troop near my house at about the same time my new church began to talk of a boy's activity and neighborhood outreach program as part of its overall ministry. The leaders were originally predisposed toward a "Royal Rangers" type of program which places heavy emphasis on Bible study and closely church-related activities. However, our church was very small and had only one boy of that age in its congregation. I was also disposed toward retaining my association with the Boy Scouts of America. I encouraged the pastor, Rev. Bill Post, that I would agree to be the head of such a boy's activity program (i.e., the Scoutmaster) should the church, after prayer, be inclined to establish a Boy Scout Troop.

By the end of that summer, the church resolved that we would indeed establish a Boy Scout Troop as the ministry of choice to neighborhood boys. We intended it as a means of ministering in the name and for the sake of Jesus Christ, with the hope that many of the boys and their families would come to know Him as a result of exposure to His Word and work in the life of the Scout troop. I began the preparation work with the Seattle Area Council and local district. I needed to obtain the minimum of five boys needed to establish a charter, as well as begin solving the various logistics problems of finding a place to meet, supplies and equipment. One of the first questions Bill asked me was, "How much money do you think we'll have to put up to enable the start of the Scout troop?"

I considered the question a moment and gave him my estimate of about $200. I explained that, until the troop had its own fund-raising program in order, it would have to commence operations with a minimum stock of equipment (tents, axes, saws, cook-kits, etc.) and supplies (notebooks, handbooks, advancement forms, training materials, pins and badges, etc.). After I provided this seemingly irrefutable reply he surprised me by saying that the church had no money and would be unable to supply any start-up financing for the troop. I thought that surely he jested; that the amount of money needed was trivial and by the time we had our minimum of five boys, we would certainly have enough funds available in the church treasury.

Time went on as, one by one, boys in the neighborhood committed to join the new troop as charter members. The very first boy was also an answer to my first prayer as prospective Scoutmaster. "Lord," I had said, "How will I possibly run this troop by myself with all new boys having no experience and no other fathers or experienced men, as well? Would you please send me an older boy with experience?" The first boy, Brian, was a 15-year-old Life Scout who had just moved into the area, having experience in canoeing, bicycling, hiking and nearly every aspect of camping and Scouting! It was not long until we had exceeded our minimum requirement of five boys and scheduled our charter meeting. All the key people were to be there, including parents, a Scout executive from the district and Pastor Post. I was still confident that by this time the church would be able to provide initial funding for the troop.

This confidence was boosted by another event which happened to coincide with this period. My wife and I had come under the conviction that we needed to be obedient to the scriptural injunction to tithe (give 10% of our income) to the church. I had decided to tithe from the date I had received Christ, some six months previously. Hence, I had only the previous week provided a check to the church for our six months' tithe. I knew the church had sufficient money to fund the troop and presumed that the pastor was informed of the church's finances.

The morning of the scheduled chartering meeting, I received a phone call at work from Pastor Post. He informed me that he had been unexpectedly called on a trip to Portland, Oregon and would be unable to attend that evening's meeting. He went immediately on to inform me that the church still had no funds with which to fund the troop. He was sorry on both points, but there didn't appear to be any solution at all to the problem of the initial financing needed for the troop. I attempted to remain outwardly calm, but was inwardly disturbed. I was also tempted, for a moment, to advise him of the fact I knew that there was money present in the church because of my tithing check. But it seemed as if my tongue were arrested. I remained silent, groaning at the prospects of attempting to initiate a troop with no funds — and also thinking that the Scout district executive would probably not permit the chartering of a troop behind which the sponsoring activity was evidently not prepared or able to stand financially. After we hung up I sat there before the Lord in bewilderment, wondering why the financial issue was proving so difficult. Would I be required to put up the money personally to enable the troop's birth?

Later the same morning I received a phone call from a man who identified himself as one of the men who worked in the local Boy Scout office. He asked me to confirm the report that I was establishing a new Scout troop and asked me," Do you need any equipment?" I replied in the affirmative and he continued, "Well, I've had this trunk full of equipment in my basement for the past couple of years, and it occurred to me that you could possibly use it for your new Scout troop." I asked him what it had in it. He said, "Well, it has some tents, saws, axes, cook kits, grills — and other things like that." I excitedly thanked him for the equipment and was easily able to make arrangements for Brian and his parents to pick it up that afternoon. I noted the way God had seemed to provide, both with respect to the equipment and to the ease of obtaining its custody, and a small light began to go on in my mind.

That evening we met in one of the Sunday School rooms of the church. The Scouting executive was there and after introductions he waved his arm toward a briefcase laying on a nearby table. "Take a look at that briefcase there and see if there's anything in it you could use." My eyes nearly popped out as I opened it and found it jammed with instructional handbooks, registration and advancement forms, and over 20 envelopes full of every type of badge and pin one could possibly imagine. I exclaimed how wonderful this would be for the troop while I continued to paw through its contents.

In another few minutes, while still investigating the briefcase, I came across an old dusty checkbook. Without thinking, I cracked the obvious joke. "Do we get to keep all the money in this account, too?" His reply was quick. "Don't laugh! That is the account of an old Scout troop that failed some time back. There's $273 still in that account. But don't get your hopes up. There are two cub packs in this area that have a prior claim on the money. Still, you could get some of it."

We commenced the evening program, the district executive presenting a movie on Scouting with some remarks, while I followed with an outline of our planned program and troop committee organization and we signed all the necessary papers for the establishment of Troop 556 of Kirkland, Washington. Then we broke up for refreshments and began to talk in various small groups. Near the end of the evening, the district executive called me over to a small group of two or three parents with which he was talking. "Karl, you won't believe this! The committee chairwoman of one of those cub packs I was telling you about is this lady here, and the treasurer of the other cub pack is this lady (both were mothers of two of our new Scouts)! They've both agreed to give all of the money in the account to your troop, provided you're agreeable to allowing any boys from those packs into this troop!"

There was never in my mind, of course, any possibility of placing conditions on any boy coming into the Scout troop. I broke into amazed exclamations of, "Praise the Lord!", clapping my hands together while practically dancing with joy and laughter as the Lord began to speak to me. "Karl, I don't need your money. I am able to provide all the resources necessary to accomplish My work. I will accomplish it by My own hand. Nor do I need your manipulations to bring it to pass, nor did I need your tithe money, as you thought I did. This is My Scout troop! What I have done this day illustrates My power to uphold My promise to meet all your needs and reveal My glory in the manner in which I do it. This is also confirmation that you are doing My work!"

How foolish my earlier anxieties now seemed. What a magnificent demonstration of God's power, lavishing upon us far beyond our projected needs. Scout troop 556 was launched with tremendous confidence that we were following God, not leading Him, in our efforts!

---
*Duff, Capt. K.M., USN, *Still the Master of the Sea*; Vantage Press, 1989.

12

Gold Nugget Camping

"...He has clothed me with garments of salvation, He has wrapped me with a robe of righteousness."

Isaiah 61:10

The first order of business for our newly chartered Scout Troop 556 was to get the boys and as many of the adults as possible trained. I had the obvious option of attempting to do this by myself, but considering that I was the only one of the church or of the parents of the Scouts who had any experience whatsoever, this "brute force" approach would take some [time? and] I was eager for alternatives. I was particularly looking for an [arrang]ement whereby I could get both the boys and the men trained in [hikin]g and camping fundamentals and give them some experience with [the leas]t waste of time and effort possible. I wanted to commence a [meaningf]ul camping program soon. Almost at once I heard about the [Ar]ea Council Gold Nugget training program.

[The Gol]d Nugget training program provided a total camping experience [to organ]ized groups of Scouts and their adults under the tutelage of [skilled] volunteer Scouters and senior Boy Scouts. The entire [event is to]tally pre-planned, with focus on use of map and compass, [setting up a p]roper camp, cooking, and other aspects of the outdoor [progra]m. The equipment and food needed by each person and [group is supplie]d and a flat fee is charged for each participant. I had never [heard of this pr]ogram before, but it sounded like just what we needed to [get started. In] November 1976, I signed up for the next Gold Nugget [event, schedule]d for January. In the meantime, I scheduled the troop [for severa]l day hikes or other day activities until we could [get started.]I promoted it among the adults and got about five [of them to signup to] the weekend concerned, as well as all of the boys.

[Early in the new]year I was at work in my office one day when it [occurred to me that we] were supposed to be scheduled for an organization [meeting]of all the units participating in the forthcoming [event. I] had heard nothing and so phoned the Council [office. The person on the oth]er end was surprised that we were uninformed. [The meeting was schedule]d that very evening; could I come? "No," I [replied]. I have iron-clad commitments with my [family tonight, but] may I have one of the other parents or men come in my place?" "Certainly!" the other Scouter replied, so I commenced my search for someone who would be available. I spent nearly the rest of the day phoning in vain all the men I could think of, including many related only with the church and having no intention of going on the campout. I then resorted to mothers, daughters and other relatives who could just represent us and illustrate that we had done our best to provide representation, but was totally unsuccessful. I was not able to find a single representative for that evening's preparation training program. Since the Gold Nugget procedures made attendance mandatory, it meant we were precluded from attending the January campout.

The following day I meditated on this and was struck with the thought that we had done our best to do all things in accordance with the Gold Nugget procedures and that our failure to be able to attend the meeting was due to no fault of our own. Even the fellow involved at the Scout office had recognized the mistake as his. We had also exhausted every possibility in attempting to respond on short notice and had run into the very unusual situation of not finding even a single person who could have attended. Yet it did not appear practical or reasonable that we defer our camping program for another two months, when the next opportunity for a Gold Nugget campout would take place. We could not put off our camping program for that long. Neither could I expect to get as many responsi[ble] fathers to sign up a second time as I had succeeded in obtaining for t[he] forthcoming one in January. Yet there was no likelihood that I co[uld] accomplish an alternative within the next two months that wo[uld] accomplish the same training level objectives. It seemed like the G[old] Nugget program was made for us and that a proper appeal would en[able] our going. I decided to phone the Scout office again.

I got the same fellow I had spoken to the previous day and outline[d the] whole situation to him, appealing to him for some alternative means [of] getting briefed and prepared so that we could attend the campout. [I was] willing to go anywhere in the Seattle area. He was adamant: "You [didn't] attend the mandatory pre-training briefing meeting and so you are [out of] the program. We're sorry, there are no exceptions made. Even th[ough it] wasn't your fault, you'll just have to wait until March." Apparently [a rule] had been invoked following some abuse of exceptions made in [the past] and there had been rigid enforcement ever since. I began to won[der what] God really had in mind for us in this situation, inasmuch as I had [reviewed] the considerations involved a number of times and could see n[othing] more promising or reasonable than the course I was pursuing. [I did] remember God's promise that He always does exceeding a[bove and] above anything that we ask or think (Eph. 3:20). About that m[oment the] man to whom I was speaking said he was willing to give me [the phone] number of the Gold Nugget Vice President if I wanted to [make an] appeal to him. I thanked him and placed the call.

In this conversation I did my best to succinctly and persuasively explain both the circumstances of our having failed to make the previous night's meeting as well as the fairly immovable set of circumstances of our new Scout troop which seemed to dictate that we obtain the Gold Nugget training right away, if at all possible. He was even more adamant than the previous man, pointing out how many times in the past it had turned into a rat race for the volunteers involved and how many times the benefitting troops had come unprepared despite the best efforts of the Gold Nugget staff. There was no hope. I began to pray that God would show me the better plan He must have for us and voiced my confidence that God must have something better since it appeared this was clearly a "closed door" for the Scout troop. Then the man offered to give me the phone number of the Gold Nugget President if I wanted to make the appeal to him. I thanked him and placed my third call.

The scenario of the conversation was the same the third time, only even more strict. The real issue was not related to why we had been unable to make the prior meeting. It was that no further exceptions were being made. By this time I was fully convinced that I was trying to batter down a closed door and resolved that I would try to find God's better alternative. I said, "Well, please don't feel badly. You have done your best and I appreciate your taking the time to explain it to me. The fact it can't be worked out is no reflection on you. It just means that God must have a better solution for my problem than we are able to see. I'll seek His solution."

Then the Gold Nugget President said, "When did you say your meeting night was?"

I responded, "Thursdays."

"And where did you say you meet?" I explained to him our meeting location in Kirkland, Washington.

"Well..." he said, "I could drive out to your troop meeting this week and give you the pre-brief in place of the scheduled troop meeting program, if you'd like. Then you could go on the campout."

My jaw dropped open in astonishment. The whole problem had just melted away! The man would come to us! We wouldn't even have to schedule or go to another special meeting! Once I had entrusted the situation to God and fully voiced my attitude of confidence in Him, it had required only a couple of sentences and a few seconds to completely resolve a situation which had resisted all prior logic and conversation.

"Praise the Lord!" I blurted out over the telephone!

Immediately there shot back to me over the earpiece, "Amen to that, brother!"

Thus did the Lord open the door for us to attend the Gold Nugget campout according to our original plan. More than this, He confirmed again that He was in our very midst. He brought me into contact with another believer and identified him in this special way to set the stage for more signs and wonders to illustrate His love for us.

The Gold Nugget Campout itself later proved to be a spectacular success, just what we needed. But God had even more immediate things to share with the Gold Nugget President.

13

A Family in Grief

"...As a garden causes the things sown in it to spring up, so the Lord God will cause righteousness and praise to spring up before all the nations."
                                                                    Isaiah 61:11

The Gold Nugget President had arrived at the Scout meeting place at our church and had set out a display perfectly designed to captivate new Scouts. Their attention was riveted to a table covered with hatchets and knives, compasses, cook kits, first aid kits, and so on, all things which pertained to our forthcoming Gold Nugget campout. They gave rapt attention to his every word. He was about 15 minutes into his presentation when Mrs. S arrived to register her son in Boy Scouting.

I had not previously met her, but had been advised some weeks earlier by a young woman in our church who had cared for her children that Mrs. S might be showing up some evening to put her son into Scouting. She had been reported to have a bad situation at home with her son also failing in school. Out of their discussion had come the recommendation that she consider our Scout troop as part of a solution to her son's problems.

However, when she arrived, the room was being used for the Gold Nugget presentation. Wanting to do nothing to distract the speaker or the boys, I suggested we talk about the procedures for registering her son in Scouting in an adjacent Sunday School room. I quickly produced a registration form, a camping equipment check-off list and summarized briefly the fees for registering, subscribing to Boy's Life and the program upon which the troop was embarked. She interrupted with, "Steve sure needs this program..." Something caught my attention regarding the depth of her cry in that statement. She was in pain. I was uncertain as to how to respond. Her son had looked perfectly normal to me in the few moments I had spent meeting him when they had entered and in seating him for the Gold Nugget briefing. I so commented to his mother and was totally unprepared for what followed.

She began to weep. In tears and convulsive sobs, she began to describe how her life was falling apart. For years her friends and relatives had been advising her to divorce her husband, an adulterer who, as her Christmas present a few weeks previously, had given her a book extolling the joys of "free love." Her son was so emotionally disturbed that he was failing school. This *very day* she had finally given up and hired a divorce lawyer.

Then she had been crushed by his callousness in the face of her family's destruction. Her world had disintegrated.

For 15 or 20 minutes she poured out her story and tears while I began to pray about what to do. I had never counselled anyone on marital problems, but I knew that God could heal a marriage. In the year or so that I had known Jesus Christ, I had seen many miracles to convince me of His power to turn destruction and despair into victory. I also discerned that this meeting was not a random occurrence. It had been divinely ordained, providing a born-again Christian to preside over the Scout meeting in the next room in order to free me to provide an answer for this woman's need. When an opportunity to speak finally came, I spoke the only conviction I had. "God can heal this marriage."

Her head lifted and we began to talk. I inquired of her attitudes toward authority, her relationship with Jesus, spoke of God's provision for her safety and protection through her husband and began to give her promises in the Bible which provide assurance of God's kind intentions and power to uphold her. I began to share my own testimony as to how God had rescued me from some terrible disasters I had been involved in the previous year. The presence of God began to pervade that room. Her faith was lifted. She began to grasp God's encouragement.

As we talked, all the unlikely events that had come together to enable our meeting began to come into focus. I would never have had opportunity to hear of the situation had we not already had in progress an unusual Scouting presentation requiring no distractions — extremely rare. Also, who but a born-again Scouter would ever understand why the Scoutmaster had disappeared for an hour to talk to a Scout mother when I had, in effect, begged him on bended knee for the Gold Nugget briefing in the first place? What a demonstration of God's love! At one point, I began to testify of my own salvation experience and then suddenly realized that this was the 13th of January, one year to the very hour of my own birth in Christ! God was celebrating my anniversary in a lavish way! He loved both of us! In our amazement in what God was doing, we began to rejoice and praise God. I suggested positive things she could do to support and encourage her husband and practical ways in which she could put her faith in God to work. We began to pray and to exult in the glory of God. Jesus was in our midst!

At precisely the moment we concluded in prayer and arose to return to the meeting, a Scout stepped to the door and said that the Gold Nugget President was requesting that I return to the meeting. It was nearly closing time! Mrs. S suddenly realized that she had demanded that her husband pack his bags and be gone when she returned home from the Scout meeting. She became frantic to find a telephone and try to stop him from departing. I believed none to be available, but as we walked out the door we tripped over a long extension-corded telephone sitting on the floor of the hallway immediately in front of our doorway. She grabbed it and succeeded in finding her husband still at home.

In my naivete, I presumed that some kind of a magic potion had been poured on Mrs. S's marriage and all aspects of her family problems had been resolved by God's intervention that evening. The marriage was restored for another ten years before it finally disintegrated in her husband's infidelity. During that time span there were many answers to prayer and on one occasion even her husband seemed to experience the Holy Spirit in his life.

But he was never delivered from the real demons that tormented him. She eventually filed for divorce. But what dramatic changes took place in her son Steve's life! Within weeks, his D's and F's in school had risen to A's and B's. His personality and attitudes were immediately altered by the prayers of that evening and Scouting. With time, he became an outstanding student and multi-talented teenager who excelled in photography, model building and art, winning state prizes in some of these categories several years running. He built his own kayak, became active in the Seattle Area Mountain Rescue Council and came to exemplify the finest points of Scouting and citizenship. When his dad finally left home, Steve became his family's source of strength and stability.

What a dramatic display of the purposeful intentions, love and power of God to intervene in our lives to bless us! God was so present! I had never before been involved in Scouting under circumstances such as these, where it was clear that the Lord was leading. We were only following. He was the real Scoutmaster.

"When (the Shepherd) puts forth all his own, he goes before them, and the sheep follow him because they know his voice" (John 10:4). These words were being fulfilled in our troop.

It made me eager for more. I wanted to find the will of God and do it to see more of His beauty!

14

A Lesson in Obedience

"But for you who fear My name the sun of righteousness will rise with healing in its wings; and you will go forth and skip about like calves from the stall."
Malachi 4:2

I frequently refer to the events of this story as a "final exam" in learning God's will through the desires of those in authority. This is not because it was my final lesson, but because it came in succession to two previous lessons under the same man in authority over me while serving in the Navy. All three incidents dealt with showing me that my attitude in supporting this man, regardless of my understanding or sympathy with his views, was essential for me to find the perfect will of God in my own life, accompanied by signs and wonders. The stories have been previously published.* However, this particular story is recounted because it also demonstrates the work God was doing through our Scout troop in Kirkland, dedicated to the work of the Lord Jesus Christ, in which He was visibly leading us from blessing to blessing.

During the summer of 1977 I had planned a nine-day High Adventure trip into the Cascade Mountains of Washington for the Scout troop, similar to those recounted in previous chapters. Everyone always considered High Adventure to be the high point of the year's schedule. It gave the boys a chance to really put into daily practice their cooking and camping skills, and to be part of a group effort. It provided a real sense of adventure and personal challenge in a wilderness environment and created stories to be remembered a lifetime. A fair amount of time in preparatory planning was invested for each of these trips.

Our trip in August 1977 involved going into the eastern part of the Cascades, hiking well into the interior, then climbing into some of the high-peaks areas and hiking out to the northern end of Lake Chelan, where we would catch a passenger ferry back to the road. We were to commence the trip on a Saturday and exit the week following on Sunday, so it was not too difficult to line up parents for the approximately 300 miles of driving required on each end of the trip.

We had to carry our own food for the duration of the nine days, which we bought and repackaged into individual patrol meals, by name and number, for each cooking group. Because of the logistics involved, it was necessary to have firm commitments and financial deposits some time prior to obtaining the food and forest service wilderness permits.

As the time for the trip approached, I began to experience difficulty in some of the preparations. First, I was informed by the forest service that, due to prolonged drought, we would be permitted no campfires, but would have to carry our own stoves. "Fine," I thought, "I've been through this one before. We'll just build charcoal stoves and prepare some paraffin-soaked charcoal. It means extra weight, but we can manage." We had about finished this chore when I was also informed that the low water levels had increased the risk of bacterial infection in the mountain streams. Being limited now in our ability to build fires and purify large quantities of water by boiling it, I decided to take some sublimed iodine crystals with me (an excellent way of purifying water for drinking without leaving significant odor or taste in the water). However, I found unexpected difficulty in obtaining the crystals.

About this time, the other adult planning to make the trip phoned to advise he would probably be unable to go because of a back injury. I had been unsuccessful in getting a third adult and so was really thrown into difficulty with this news, inasmuch as a minimum of two adults was required under any circumstances. After a few days of seeking the Lord in the matter and many dozens of unsuccessful phone calls seeking a third adult, Fred called me again to confirm doctor's orders that he would not be allowed to make the trip.

Now I was in serious straits. What was I to do? Postpone the trip? We had spent months planning it. Dates and leave schedules had been set nine months earlier. Family vacations, transportation and all sorts of details in many different families were now all fixed, based on this schedule. No, I could not postpone it. I'd just have to find another adult willing to make the trip. About that time I received a call from a friend of a friend visiting from Maine. He was in town for a few weeks and had been asked to call me to say hello. He was 18 years old and had never been camping, much less backpacking. Was he interested? Well, maybe. I borrowed a set of boots and took him out for a stiff trek in the mountains on the weekend prior to our scheduled departure. He came back with blisters and totally worn out, but was willing to go on the trip. "Well," I thought, "he doesn't offer much strength in case of an emergency, but he meets the letter of the law. He'll count as a second adult and the trip can go on."

Nevertheless, by this time I was seriously questioning God as to what was going on. Things didn't feel right. I didn't feel comfortable with the weakness in adult supervision. Parents were calling me, telling me that their boys had colds and they didn't know if they should let them go on the trip. And my iodine crystals still hadn't come in. "Lord," I asked, "why is this so hard? What are You doing? What is it You want me to do?" I couldn't seem to get any answer. So I continued on my plans to depart Saturday morning.

On Thursday morning, just two days before departure, I made another inquiry on the arrival of the iodine crystals. I was told they wouldn't be arriving until the following Monday! I was upset; why wouldn't things fall into place? Again I considered delaying the trip, but the thought of the difficulties in rescheduling everything for everyone involved overwhelmed me. We were committed to go, iodine crystals or not.

Later Thursday morning I was on the phone in one of my daily phone conversations with my boss, a Navy Captain, in Washington, D.C. During the conversation he casually mentioned something he wanted me to do the following Monday. My alarms went off. "But Captain, I'm supposed to be on leave next week, remember?"

"Oh, yes," he replied, "I forgot about that. But, anyway, here's what I want you to do next Monday...."

"Captain, you don't understand. I'm involved with nearly a dozen different families, taking their sons into the mountains. I can't just call them up and tell them to forget it! We've spent months planning this thing."

"Well," he said, "How about postponing it by five days? I think you can finish up what I want done by Wednesday."

"Captain," I said, "We've got parents committed to drive on weekends. If I postpone five days, they'll have to drive 300 miles on a workday. Some boys will probably have to drop out. I don't see how I can postpone it."

"Okay," said the Captain, "You go ahead and do what you think is right. But you know what I want you to do!" That ended our conversation, but by this time my heart was singing, for I knew I had received clear direction from the Lord. Now, if only He would enable me to execute His directions without further difficulty.

"Lord, if it is Your will to postpone this trip by five days, please confirm it by enabling me to make alternative transportation arrangements without any difficulty. Thank you. Amen."

Starting from scratch, without any work phone numbers or any knowledge of where the fathers or mothers worked, and lacking even a troop roster of home phone numbers in my immediate possession, I was able to rearrange transportation for our entire party to depart on a Thursday morning and return on a Friday afternoon, all arrangements completed within 30 minutes. It proved to be much simpler, by far, than the original arrangements made weeks before. I began to pray to God, "Lord, I know You are doing something wonderful. Please show me what it is!"

By Saturday, the day we would have departed, had we not postponed, storm clouds had moved in and rains began to pour down; gully-washing, persistent, day after day heavy rain. "Wow!" I thought. "Am I ever glad we are not out in that rain!" (In fact, it was snow in the high mountains.)

On Sunday I arose in church to announce that God had directed that we postpone our nine-day trip by five days and asked that the congregation pray for God to reveal His purposes for the delay.

On Monday, I went to work as directed, commenced the effort my Captain had requested (and picked up the iodine crystals!). Late in the morning I received a call from one of the most harassed and hard-working mothers in the troop, one for whom I had previously been praying because of the demands placed on her by her three boys, all of whom were in the Scout troop. She spoke in a voice filled with despair and depression, "I'm afraid the boys won't be able to go on the trip, now." (For an instant I angrily thought, "What now? Another set of colds? We should have left last Saturday, after all!" I am ashamed to confess these thoughts.) She continued on, "Their father, Russ, was in a bad accident last night and is in critical condition with a broken back!"

God knows the flood of grief and anguish I felt for this woman, who had always seemed to me to have to struggle excessively to satisfy her sons, now facing the loss of her husband. I was abashed at my angry thoughts of a few moments earlier, mumbled some condolences and hung up thinking "God, You've got to do something about this. This is just not satisfactory for that lady. We've got to help her." I prayed for awhile and then thought of calling my pastor, Bill Post, and suggesting we pray together. The call was successful and he went immediately afterwards to the hospital. For that day, and Tuesday and Wednesday, as well, Russ Walden was visited at his bedside and prayed for by either our pastor or one of our assistant pastors.

In the meantime, my brother, Larry, an experienced mountaineer, discovered quite by "accident" that we had postponed our trip by five days and he was now able to go with us! This solved the weakness in the adult leadership. Also, the rains continued to pour down.

On Thursday, we commenced our trek into the mountains. The skies were cool and grey. The rains seemed to have let up just for us and we had only a light drizzle as we hiked in through the forest. We had only gone a couple of miles when we came to a party headed out the other way. "How has it been?" we asked.

"Terrible!" they replied. "It has done nothing but pour down rain on us for five straight days! We were originally planning on a whole week, but we've given up. We quit!"

"There but for obedience to the voice of God, goes us," thought I. Nor was the lesson lost on my brother.

The whole rest of that trip was enchanted. It was as though rain was not allowed to fall on us. Though there was rain the entire trip, it never rained on us while we were hiking, and we hiked over fifty miles. The only times it rained were when we had set up camp and were in our tents. On four or five occasions, the first drops fell just as the last stake was driven, or just as we entered camp after an all-day hike. Our charcoal stoves enabled us to do all our cooking under the rain flies, even though the fire ban had obviously ended. On the days we had planned to visit the high-peaks areas, we had delightful weather, which held for the entire day, turning to rain only as our feet actually entered the campsite upon our return.

On the last two days we actually had rain clouds follow us down the trail, then onto the ferry boat, down the lake, and back to the cars. Ten minutes after the cars were packed and we were on our way, we were in a downpour.

The whole trip was as delightful and enchanted an experience in harmony with nature as I have ever experienced. I praised the Lord continually throughout the entire trip.

Returning home to Seattle, I faced the $64.00 question, "How was Russ Walden?" I called his home and the youngest son told me he was fine, that he really hadn't broken his back after all! I hung up, puzzled and with mixed feelings. "God, I guess that a mistake by the doctors is one way of answering a prayer. But, in that case, why wouldn't it have been better for the boys to have gone on the trip?" I set the matter aside until the next Scout meeting, when I saw Mrs. Walden personally.

"How's Russ?" I asked.

"Oh, fine," she said, "The only real problem he had was when they drilled the holes in his head!"

"What?" I exclaimed, "Do you mean they actually drilled holes in his head and placed him in traction before they discovered their mistake?"

"Well, the doctors don't believe they made a mistake," said Mrs. Walden. "On Sunday night when they brought him into emergency treatment and on Monday when they placed him in traction, they took a total of seventeen X-rays. They all showed a clean break. On Thursday morning (the day our trip had commenced) they took another set of X-rays and they showed no break whatsoever! When the doctor called me in to try to explain, he just said, 'I can't explain this, Mrs. Walden. Here's two sets of X-rays that show a break. But these latest show none at all. I can't explain it.' So, "they cut him down and sent him home."

God had arranged that conversation to include Mrs. S, the precious Scout mother who had given her heart to Christ. We stood there together, soaking in the realization of what God had done, and my heart witnessed to me that this was what God had been about all along — to heal and bring an entire family to Christ. "God opposes the proud, but gives grace to the humble." He had answered my prayer to show me His purposes in the delay of the trip without which this man would have never come under our prayers.

The whole incident was one which was available by a path visible only to one willing to recognize and follow the voice of God speaking through someone in authority; yes, even someone seemingly unreasonable.

God knows exactly my skeptical mind. He knows I would have always been doubtful either that the doctors and technicians who took those X-rays had done their jobs properly or that Mrs. Walden had reported it correctly. But, as chance would have it, one of our assistant pastors, who supported himself as a radiological (X-ray) technician, had been on duty at the hospital the night Russ was brought in. He was an eyewitness to the X-rays!

---

*Duff, Capt. K.M., USN, *Still the Master of the Sea*; Vantage Press, 1989.

A Lesson in Obedience 69

**Wading the Entiat River, North Cascades
Washington High Adventure — 1977**

**Summit, Buckskin Mountain, 8100 Feet.
North Cascades High Adventure — 1977**

15

Boys Without Fathers

"The Lord protects the strangers; He supports the fatherless and the widow..."
Psalm 146:9

When I began adult Scouting in the early 1960s, the typical Scout family had both a mother and father. Now about half the boys come from broken homes and about one third of the Scouts I have worked with over the past ten years have had no fathers. A few fathers have been deceased, but the majority have been lost through divorce. The results on their sons are marked. I believe most sociologists who claim that divorce does not leave permanent damage on children must have little long-term or personal work with such children at the teenage level.

Most teenage boys are stronger willed than their mothers. Mothers are usually not able or willing to bear the emotional brunt of applying the level of accountability and discipline that a boy needs to develop security and stable emotional behavior. Boys generally develop a variety of methods for getting their way, frequently involving emotional extremes. With their mothers, they become accustomed to getting away with this and with having less consistent and rigidly applied standards of behavior than do boys with fathers. In addition, the mothers themselves sometimes have their own emotional problems which either contributed to or resulted from the failure of the marriage, and which tend to be passed on to the children. These combined effects are especially detrimental for an adolescent boy experiencing puberty, trying to find his identity as a man and exposed to a variety of destructive influences in a rebellious teenage world. Combined with resentment, false guilt and the loss of self worth that a boy usually has when his parents separate, a family without a father in authority produces a boy who is difficult to work with, yet who is subconsciously screaming for someone willing to do so.

The trend has been continuous and is worsening. Extremes of behavior seem to get worse year by year. Anger, viciousness, rebellion, resentment, paranoia and deficiencies in the areas of values and motivation make it more and more difficult to work effectively with such boys. Meanwhile, the number of fathers who are available and willing to do so is steadily shrinking. It is perhaps one measure of the progressive destruction taking place in the American family and in our society. We are losing our manhood.

So a relevant question is, what are effective methods for dealing with disciplinary problems in boys and with problem boys in particular? Do they follow common themes and principles which are transferable? Necessity has forced a search for such principles. I believe I have discovered some and offer them here. Although necessity was driven by "problem" boys, the principles apply to all.

The most important principle in working with boys is to understand that men who so serve do so only as agents of the parents; i.e., to support parents in raising their sons. They are assisting in what parents are already attempting to achieve, and parents are God's chief authorities over their children. This includes single parents. Nearly every point to be made here (or the manner in which it was discovered) is undergirded by the fact that it is really parents who have the task, the vision, the desire, the wisdom and authority to raise up their sons, and even if they have made a mess of it, they will rise to the occasion when given opportunity to work with someone who honors their preeminence as God's agents over their children.

It is important, too, to recognize that Boy Scouting already occupies the major arena of true interest of parents: the development of character, citizenship and physical fitness of their sons. Though not always well articulated, Boy Scouting is light years ahead of sports, music, drama, debate and a host of other activities which develop important skills, but not in the sense of building overall character, citizenship and fitness. Parents carry a vision of their sons that extends beyond obvious hope for their happiness and the subsequent raising of grandchildren. They desire their children to find satisfaction, esteem and fulfillment in their work and families. They desire regard by others for their children because of their characters, accomplishments and reputations; effectiveness in working for good, not only in their families, but in their communities. The foundational strength of Scouting is that it provides the opportunity for boys to grow into manhood in an environment which fosters growth of these qualities in a manner few other programs can, while introducing each Scout to a host of activities and skills which give him opportunity to discover his major talents and interests beyond levels which most families could ever pursue individually.

This will not satisfy the father who wants his boy to be a big league baseball star, or who is convinced that competitive sports is the only pathway to manhood. Nor will it resolve the conflict a mother has with a son who has already decided that he will do only what his friends do, even if that is nothing in particular. It will not develop an expert skier, musician or scholar. But it will expose and develop a well-rounded young man with a variety of interests and skills, a knowledge of how to accomplish worthwhile goals through cooperative effort and a well-developed conscience that can discern right from wrong with potentially enough courage to act accordingly. In addition, it yields a rich background of experience and friendships that have grown and survived a fair number of difficult trials over several years. The substance of faithfulness (i.e., trustworthy-ness and loyal-ty, the first two Scout Laws) is built in a manner that gives it real meaning. An older Scout can discern it and appreciate it in others. He takes it with him when he leaves Scouting and will look for it in marriage and employment relationships. It is also noteworthy that it is the boys who reach the top rung of the Scouting ladder, Eagle Scout, who usually have the combinations of achievements in other areas, including the athletics, music, drama, debating, student government and skills mentioned above which mark outstanding performers.

So, given the attributes of Scouting and the fact that it squarely aligns with the primary motivation of parents in their aspirations for their sons, what conclusions should we draw regarding how to deal with the problems of difficult boys? I suggest the following:

(1) Parents are the ultimate authority in disciplining their children (short of violation of the civil or criminal law).

(2) Standards which are to be enforced must have the endorsement of parents in order to be ultimately enforceable.

(3) Parents will provide right standards when they know your purpose is to support them in their sons' lives. Parents' standards will usually be as strict as the Scout leader's, as well as being in compliance with the Scout Law. This is true even if the parent has never previously provided standards in a particular area.

(4) A Scout who is disciplined by the Scoutmaster for violating his parents' standards and whose parents and Scoutmaster are working cooperatively must respond or face the pain of further discipline. He has no place to hide.

Given these undergirding fundamentals, the remaining precepts are quite simple, although they require considerable discipline on part of the leaders to apply. They include:

(5) Food and fellowship are the most powerful life-support activities that a boy has. Removal of food or fellowship are the most powerful means of discipline.

(6) Admission of error (agreement on the truth) and a request for forgiveness from those offended is helpful in building a positive experience and lasting lesson out of major disciplinary problems.

(7) Parents are excellent judges of when their sons have learned their lessons and should serve as chief counsellors in structuring restoration of sons to fellowship.

Application of these principles is a growth experience for the Scoutmaster. It obliges him to be accountable to parents for his attitudes and standards. Before he approaches parents to make an appeal to them regarding a Scout's behavior, he is forced to review his own actions and words. In the melee of action among a group of men and boys there is frequently ample need for correction of the Scoutmaster's own attitudes and actions. Also, there is great reinforcement in the attitude he is trying to instill in the Scout *by his own example of submission to the Scout's parents*. The boy will be impressed by the example of someone outside his family honoring his parents (although at the same time he is doubly wishing he hadn't pushed the Scoutmaster so far)!

There is a hidden prerequisite, though, which stands as a paramount precept. Scouting requires volunteer men willing to serve. Within this precept itself are the basic, most important seeds of success. (Conversely, without men willing to serve, all talk about other principles is mere vapor.) Yes, precepts of discipline are important, but they all pale next to the prerequisite of men willing to serve boys! If men will make themselves available, solutions to problems and learning will follow naturally.

There are practically no qualifications necessary for a man to be successful in teaching and leading boys aside from having basically pure motives and a willingness to serve. Men come fully equipped in the most vitally needed qualification, inherent authority and the natural regard and respect that a man carries with a boy. This is almost unique among all the areas of service which a man could consider; something almost no other job could offer. Boys are naturally willing to presume competence and follow a man willing to lead. The man will have almost no problem in generating motivation if he is simply available. Further, he usually has sufficient experience regarding the principles of cooperative group effort to be able to lead young Scouts.

Manhood is fundamentally built upon the need for men living and giving their life on behalf of women and children. A man willing to submit his life in service to boys can be assured that in his very service he will spread the seed of manhood. Because many men do not know this and serve other priorities and fears, they pass up many rich rewards. "As you sow, so you shall reap" (Gal. 6:7-9).

In the application of major discipline for problem Scouts, I have found that several weeks of suspension from all troop activities, followed by a written and public apology (involving only those who were involved in the offense), provides extensive behavioral correction. A written apology is needed to thoroughly test the Scout's spirit of repentance and understanding of specific actions for which he is really apologizing before he stands in front of those he offended.

Removal of food is especially effective in campout situations where significant removal from fellowship is impractical or not an immediate option. In situations where denial of all food is impractical or ill-advised (such as on a strenuous hike trip), denial of dessert produces amazingly powerful results. In fact, I would say that no discipline gets a boy's attention and can provoke him to such prodigious levels of objection, counter-charges, negotiation and promised behavioral change as the removal of dessert privileges!

An advantage of a solid Scouting program containing plenty of challenge, strong adult support and opportunity for new accomplishments for Scouts, is that it supports the building of a solid relationship between Scout and Scoutmaster which is capable of bearing the heavy load of discipline. A Scout needs to know that the Scoutmaster is on his side; he is sincerely concerned for him and is consistently working on his behalf. Occasionally the need for strong discipline arises before such a solid relationship can be built and a boy will flee the discipline. But if the Scoutmaster is faithful to apply consistent standards, assures that he works without partiality and yields his own interests to the needs of his Scouts, he can be confident his Scouts will discern that he is indeed their friend and respond accordingly. Times of discipline can become one of the most rewarding parts of the Scoutmaster/Scout relationship.

On one occasion, immediately following suspension of a difficult Scout for a 30-day period, I spent some time with him explaining to him how he could be confident that I really cared for him and was working on his behalf; that if he had never been confident of it before, he could be confident now. He naturally was curious and I explained to him from the Scriptures: "My son, do not reject the discipline of the LORD, or loathe His reproof, for whom the LORD loves, he reproves, even as a father, the son in whom he delights" (Prov. 3:11-12). Then I followed with Scriptures from Hebrews (12:7-11), explaining that his being disciplined was the proof that he was a "legitimate son rather than illegitimate" and giving him the promise that it would bear the "peaceful fruit of righteousness." Later in the day, I called his mother to advise her of the action and submit some of the administrative issues to her. I was surprised to hear her play back to me the words I had shared with her son, which he had already shared with her almost word for word. He had displayed to her a good attitude over his being disciplined and had been especially impressed with the fact that this was proof that he was loved as a son. He had had no father in his family for many years.

On several occasions, I have contacted parents to advise them that their son is violating some situation within the troop or has offended other parents. I have asked them to give me a statement of their standards for their son for these situations and promised them I would enforce their standards. I have never failed to receive the fullest cooperation and support from each of the parents involved and achieve significant behavioral improvement in the Scout.

In one situation involving fighting, I held a meeting with both of the fathers and Scouts present and asked the fathers to resolve what their standards were for their boys. We wrote down the standards and the consequences that would occur if the standards were violated and never had another conflict between the two boys.

On another occasion, a difficult boy (again, with no father) behaved obscenely while being given a ride home by a second Scout's mother. She was so angry at the Scout she refused to let him in her car again. I suggested that I have the offending Scout's mother call her and be given the story first-hand so that she could have opportunity to give her son correct standards. When the second mother agreed, I made the call to the Scout's mother, gave only a brief outline of the situation and told her I would support her in whatever action she decided to take after informing herself of the true facts and would uphold her standards of behavior for her son in this situation. Her response was so powerful and complete that we never had another problem in that area with her son, and his general behavior improved also.

The most difficult disciplinary situation I have faced is one for which the story is still incomplete. A Scout named Chester had been in the troop for four years and had had no father for most of that time. He had a long history of hyperactivity and anger which was frequently barely under control, even under normal circumstances. Often he would become unmanageable, destroying his equipment, venting his anger in shouting and disobedience and becoming intolerable to the other Scouts. As he grew older he began to run around at school with bad friends, to smoke, drink and experiment with drugs. About this time his mother remarried and he came under the stronger control of his step-father, but Chester decided against accepting his parents' discipline and moved out of the house. I happened to find out about it by phoning while he was actually packing his bags and finding his mother in tears!

I prayed about it and decided that the Scout Oath and Law required me to do my best in upholding the standards which Chester's parents were attempting to hold before Chester; that failure to support them while he was in flagrant violation of their authority would be a false pretense that nothing was wrong in Chester's Scouting life when things were actually very wrong! So, with prior notice to his parents, I wrote a short letter to Chester outlining the areas of the Scout Oath and Law where I thought he was in violation by his failure to accept his parents' authority and suspended him indefinitely from the Scout troop. A week later he lay paralyzed in a local hospital's intensive care unit as a result of having taken amphetamines while intoxicated on alcohol.

The events following Chester's brush with death were traumatic; they were a time of prayer, counsel and introspection. He made a successful physical recovery and was placed on a path of drug rehabilitation amid hopes for life changes in his attitudes and habits. So far the story of Chester's rehabilitation is one of answered prayer and the grace of God. Months in private and state drug treatment facilities helped him gain control of his emotions; he has drawn closer to His confessed Savior Jesus Christ and returned to public school. He came back to the Scout troop. Changes seem to have taken place. But who can explain God's work completely? And who knows what roads lie ahead for Chester as he makes his way through life? In this case, it is difficult to say the extent to which obedience helped God to work, or whether it is His grace that has covered our mistakes. The pathway we walk is painful. Offering these precepts to volunteers is clearly not a formula for cheap and easy victories. They are "two-edged" and require growth in the Scout leader as well as in the Scout. However, to anyone willing to try to uphold them, they will produce victories that make the effort worthwhile.

16

An Adventure in Forgiveness — Part I

"The mind of man plans his way, but the LORD directs his steps."
Proverbs 16:9

My son Kenneth was 8 years old in 1978 when I was transferred by the Navy from Seattle, Washington back to Washington, D.C. for duty. We had rented out our home in Alexandria during our absence, anticipating our possible return. In June of 1978 we moved back into our old neighborhood, but I had no plans to continuing in Boy Scouting with my former troop. It was my intention to become active with Kenny in Cub Scouting and then possibly move back into a Scout troop when he became eligible to graduate from Cubbing to Boy Scouting.

We had been back in town only a few days when I made contact with some of the members of my old Troop 659. I found that it had been lacking a Scoutmaster for some four or five months. I also discovered that the other troop sponsored by that same church had lost its Scoutmaster for a similar period. There had been no camping program, nor had either troop sent any boys to summer camp that summer. Weekly meetings of both troops had also been terminated. Both were essentially defunct.

Surprisingly, there were still six or eight boys registered in Troop 659 which I had initiated into Scouting; of course they were quite a bit bigger and more mature than when I had last seen them. Few new boys had been brought in during the three-year interim. The "veterans" were eager to continue a program. Naturally, there was a strong appeal made to me by the boys and their fathers that I take over the troop again as Scoutmaster. I declined, explaining my plans to be active in Cub Scouting with my son. However, I said I would help train one of the fathers if he would take the job and that I would also support an occasional campout. No one stepped forward immediately.

During the month of July, the men of the troop met once or twice to discuss various cooperative approaches by which leadership could be restored and a program established. I exhorted and encouraged the fathers, whom I knew fairly well from our earlier relationship, that they certainly could handle the job if they would support each other, but we didn't seem to be able to get a man who would serve as Scoutmaster. Near the end of the month we scheduled another meeting down at the Scout hut to discuss the matter further. Or so I thought.

I arrived a few minutes early on a lovely Thursday evening and sat down on the grass to await the other arrivals. The sun was still well up in the sky and I had ample opportunity to view the beauty of the surroundings and contemplate anything that might come to mind. I began to muse over the Scout troop situation when suddenly God spoke to me.

"Karl, you should consider taking over this Scout troop again, provided you can make it into a ministry for Me, like the one you had in Seattle!"

It does little good to attempt explaining to a third party how one knows he has just been spoken to by the Lord. One of the reasons I think it may be so difficult is that the hearer's instant astonishment and amazement is also nearly immediately mixed with some degree of his own doubt and questioning; "How do you know this was from the Lord, and not your own thoughts?" God seems to have a way of taking this into account and leading each of His children in a manner suitable to vindicate and confirm His words to them. In this case, my amazement was sufficient to cause me to abandon my rigid position of refusing to serve as Scoutmaster and begin a review of what the Lord might have in mind, even while questioning how God might authenticate that He had indeed spoken to me.

The immediate problems I faced as I began my review were as follows: First, I was not a member of this church as I had been in Seattle when that Scout troop was formed. My family and I had already been directed to another church up the street and we had no doubt that we had been accurately directed. Second, this troop was already established. I had no idea what the views of the sponsoring church were regarding Boy Scouting, but I imagined it was far distant from the view we had in Seattle, where the primary intention was to reach boys for the Kingdom of God and enable their salvation through Jesus Christ. Third, I doubted the sponsoring church was a believer in many of the gifts of the Holy Spirit to the extent of my church in Seattle and that it was not likely that they could operate here in the spectacular manner that they had within the Seattle troop. I also was aware that there had to be a line of accountability and spiritual authority all the way down from the head of the church to me in order for the blessings of God to flow to us. I had no idea what the line of spiritual authority within this church was.

I began to consider how I would approach the matter if I were to lay out a plan to proceed. I would have to seek out and place myself under the church authority structure under which I would operate. I would have to establish harmony and unity of spirit regarding the goals of the Scout troop. I would have to seek prayer and blessing of the church authorities. I would have to... Suddenly, the thought came rushing through like a sword searing my insides — "I will have to reconcile myself for the ugly letter I wrote over four years ago to the men's club, breaking off relationships with them. I will have to apologize and ask their forgiveness!"

The force of this thought threw me back onto the grass in agony. Why would I have to go back and open up something which had happened so long ago? Why was it necessary at all, considering the fact that it was we who had been wronged? Perhaps the men's club wasn't in the line of church authority, anyway. Why was the thought of seeking forgiveness over this matter so painful? I groaned over the prospect and began to cling to the idea that these were my own thoughts and not the Lord, at all.

Fifteen or twenty minutes had elapsed and no one had shown up for the meeting I thought we had scheduled. The church parking lot was empty and I was totally alone. I continued to wrestle with my problem. Why did I need to seek forgiveness? Everything else it appeared I would have to do was reasonable and fairly direct; God would give me guidance as I moved ahead. I felt I could forgive and forget what the men's club had done to us. But to take responsibility for my sin and seek their forgiveness seemed too painful to contemplate. God was telling me to get serious about making things right in my past and even as I groaned over it, I knew the unmistakable hand of the Lord.

At that moment my ear was unusually alerted to the sound of a car driving down Franconia Road, some 100 yards away, slowing to enter the parking lot. The Lord indicated to me who the driver was even before the car came into sight from behind the trees. It was a word of knowledge from the Lord. Again there came the question as to whether this was really from God.

The car rounded the corner into the driveway, past the front lawn and into the parking lot toward me while I squinted my eyes to confirm who it was. He drove up near me and got out of the car. It was Bill Yehle, the former Scoutmaster of the other Scout troop and the man who had been my troop counterpart when I had written the ugly letter four years earlier. I was dumbfounded that he was the man whom God had just identified to me in His word of knowledge. Now all doubt regarding the author of this conversation and the direction I had received vanished.

I jumped up, not having seen Bill in over four years. I excitedly told him of what God had just done in encouraging me to take Troop 659 over again and broached the subject as to whether or not he might feel led to consider taking over Troop 1150 also. I talked about making the troops into an outreach for the Lord Jesus Christ and broached the subject of my ugly letter with the opinion that I needed to be forgiven for it. I think my enthusiasm washed out any caution I could have had and he was somewhat taken aback. However, he indicated some interest and seemed to welcome an opportunity to think things over when I told him I wanted to pray about the matter for a few days and discuss it with my wife. He said he would do likewise.

By this time it was quite clear that either I had misunderstood the intention of the troop's fathers to hold a meeting at the Scout hut, or that for some reason they had all decided not to show up. I went home, made some phone calls and determined that I was the only one who had thought there was such a meeting. I passed the word I was reconsidering the possibility of acting as the Troop 659 Scoutmaster.

A week or so later, I was sitting at the kitchen table with my wife, Gretchen, when I suddenly became agitated and restless in my spirit. I had a strong urging to go down to the church parking lot and spend some time there, for what reason I did not know. This seemed quite irrational to me, inasmuch as there were no meetings planned of which I knew, nor was the day of the week one on which Scout or church activities normally took place. Nor had I ever previously received or followed such "off the wall" urgings. I resisted it, but after a few more minutes I announced to Gretchen that I felt I needed to drive down to the church for a little while and if nothing happened, I would be home shortly. I drove into the empty parking lot, parked and began to pray, focusing upon the events of the previous week and asking God for definitive direction.

After about 25 minutes of prayer, I sat back, looked at my watch, thanked God for calling me down there for some dedicated prayer and asked if there was any other reason for my being there. I got no answer. I decided an even half hour seemed to be a good round number for this uncertain quest and told the Lord that if nothing more happened in the half hour, I would head on home. Three or four more minutes passed.

About the time I was deciding to turn on the ignition key and start home, I heard an automobile come down Franconia Road and turn into the parking lot behind me. I knew immediately who it was. It was, indeed, Bill Yehle who drove up next to me, got out wearing his Scouter's shirt and announced that he had been sitting at home, when he suddenly decided that he needed to retake his Scoutmaster's position in the other troop. He had thrown on his Scout shirt and immediately driven down to the church to open the Scout hut and start work!

I shared with Bill what had just happened to me and my conviction that I was required to provide an apology and request for forgiveness to the men's club for my letter of years before. I suggested that he might want to join me. The strength of his reply surprised me; he made it clear that I was on my own. I dropped the matter with him, but with no further uncertainty as to what was required of me.

Thus was set in motion a tortuous search in finding the will of God in the matter of seeking forgiveness on an issue vital to gaining the release of God's power in the Scout troop He had asked me to lead again. Before finding His answers, I would be nearly desperate in my hunger to see evidence of His presence in our midst.

17

An Adventure in Forgiveness — Part II

"Truly I say to you, whatever you shall bind on earth shall be bound in heaven; and whatever you loose on earth shall be loosed in heaven."
                                                               Matthew 18:18

In August 1978 I again became Scoutmaster of Troop 659 and began to implement a camping and training program while proceeding at once to search out the best manner to accomplish what God had set before me: making this troop a ministry for the Lord, like the one in Seattle. My first appointment for counsel and direction was with the church pastor.

At the appointed time I met with him in his church office and described to him the full story of how I had come to Christ a few years earlier and of the miracles He had done in my life, especially in the Seattle area Scout troop which had been established in His name. I described the miracles of finances, supply, healing, ministry to marriages and personal salvation which we had seen as the Lord moved ahead of us. Then I did my best to summarize the directions I thought I had received in the immediate preceding weeks, with special emphasis on the need for a formal request for forgiveness by the men's club for the letter I had written in early 1974.

The gentlemanly pastor heard me through, but I had the feeling that my words were not penetrating. There seemed to be no power to my testimony, as though I were speaking against walls of brass. At my conclusion, he graciously agreed to place his blessing on the Scout troop, and to pray for us, as well as to pass the report onto the Council of Ministry of the church which was responsible for the outreach of the church body. Then he said, "But there's no need for you to apologize to the men's club. They are not a part of our outreach program and they have no direct line in our ministry efforts, anyway. I think its best if you just forget the incident regarding your letter to them."

With surprise and a great inward sigh of relief I welcomed his decision, even while doubting that he was being responsive to God's direction. I was off the hook and would not have to face the dreaded task of apologizing in front of the men's club!

Wasn't this pastor God's authority in this church? Couldn't I be confident that I had heard from God through him? But what if he was wrong? Would I hear from God again on the subject? How could I have got so mixed up in confusing God's direction to me? We concluded in prayer and I left with a mixture of relief that I had accomplished what I came to do and some misgivings that perhaps the one from whom I had expected to receive definitive direction was not hearing from God.

Fall and winter of 1978 came and the troop worked its way back into the routine of meetings, activities and campouts. The trouble was, there was no evidence of the Lord's presence. Yes, we had protection from mishaps, solutions to our financial needs, and normal activity for Scout troops, but none of the mind-boggling, beautiful work of the Lord which had so typified much of the everyday activity of the troop in Seattle. I was troubled. I needed to see the Lord's presence. I wanted the boys to see Him. I had been tasked by the Lord to "...make it into a ministry for (Him), like the one in Seattle." What had I done wrong? Was it possible that I had been disobedient in not carrying out the Lord's instructions regarding the apology? The thought was frequent and recurring. I was reasonably sure that this was the cause of the problem, but leaned on the principle that it was God's responsibility to make His definitive will to me made known through the authorities He placed over me.

In the meantime, the relationship of benign neglect which I had seen years before continued unabated. Never did I see a single man of the church near the Scout hut or any expression of interest whatsoever in their activities. The Scout hut itself was a constant series of problems with lights, winter heating, water and maintenance.

Early in 1979, the pastor of the church was replaced with a new pastor. The thought struck me that this was a bit unusual but it was timely from my standpoint because it gave me another opportunity to visit with the new pastor and resubmit the whole issue to his leadership and counsel. I thought, "If the first pastor got it wrong, then surely God will straighten it out through this one." By this time, I had a great sense of urgency to correcting whatever the unseen matter was that was blocking the release of God's power into the ministry of the Scout troop.

So I made an appointment to visit with the new pastor. It was almost a replay of the meeting with the previous pastor; skies of brass, no illumination in the testimony, no power in the prayer and, most significantly, no change in direction regarding the pastor's dismissal of any need to carry out an apology for the ugly letter of five years earlier. Again, I felt the relief of knowing that I would not have to carry out this unpleasant task (which I was really dreading), but I had a heavy heart as I left, being almost convinced that this man was also not hearing from the Lord, to whom I was eager to submit.

Spring and summer of 1979 followed and the troop was like a desert. With only one minor exception (Chapter 28), we did not have a single incident that illustrated the power or love of God happen in our midst. I was grieved. How frequently I sought the Lord, with the question, "Lord,

An Adventure in Forgiveness — Part II   85

why is it You are not in our midst? Have I been disobedient? What must I do to open the way for Your presence among us? Have I not been obedient to those who you've placed in authority over this church? What more can I do?"

After a six-month term in office, the new pastor was suddenly dismissed by the church without a replacement. His precipitous removal was over matters to which I was not privy. However, it was evident by now that there seemed to be a cycle of removal of pastors that might possibly be related to the issue of whether or not they were giving godly counsel to those who were seeking it. I eagerly called up the church again to see if I could get an appointment with whoever it was that was acting as the new church pastor, but found that there was no one acting in such authority and that their Sunday services were being supported by a series of guest speakers and visiting pastors. So I continued to cool my heels, fretting and agitating over the issue and seeming to get nowhere in my prayers.

One day in November 1979, I came home from work and Gretchen pointed out to me a phone message. "You were called by so-in-so from the Methodist Church men's club. They want to know if you'll participate in this year's Christmas Tree sale!"

The reader will just have to imagine as best he can the shrivelling force of her words. All my Scouting efforts and prayers of nearly a year and a half came into focus in that single statement. God was calling me to reconcile the issue of my relationship with that men's club. I recoiled as if I had been struck with a baseball bat. Frozen by fear, I ducked the issue and hoped they would forget to call again! My mind was almost continuously preoccupied with this thought for the next couple of days.

A few days later I came home and Gretchen said to me again, "So-in-so called from the Methodist Church men's club again. They want your answer about the Christmas Tree sale tonight." I could not escape. I had to do something. I was in agony for direction.

I went down to my basement recreation room and began to pace the floor, revisiting the same questions over which I had poured out prayer for a year and a half. "Lord, what is it You want me to do? Have I not been obedient? Is my failure to carry my apology to the men's club the reason You have not been present in the Scout troop? Why can't I see You in the Scout work? You know I sincerely want to see You. How could it be that You could not give me consistent direction through those whom You have placed in authority over the church? Is that the reason they have been removed from office? What do You want me to do?" For a number of minutes I paced the floor, practically shouting these questions at the Lord in desperation in my spirit. I had completed these series of questions for the third time when the Lord spoke to me.

It was the first time He had spoken to me in such a manner since that sunny afternoon nearly 17 months earlier when He had given me direction with respect to the Scout troop. Now He said, "Karl, you got it wrong the first two times. Are you going to get it right the third time?"

POW! My response was instantaneous! I had heard from the Lord! I slammed my hand into my fist and resolved in that moment to carry out His directions immediately. Now the question was how to do it. Who did I know whom I could even call? Who would understand? I needed to call someone immediately and arrange to get in front of the men's club!

A name and face came immediately to mind. During the previous year we had had an Eagle Scout Court of Honor for one of our Scouts. At it a kindly older gentleman named Billy Gray, our Scouting Coordinator at the time, had spoken a few words in honor of the Scout. In his words he had made it evident that he treasured his relationship with his Savior, Jesus Christ. It was clear he knew the Lord and was looking forward to seeing Him face to face. I knew he would be able to help me if I could just find out how to contact him. I started across the basement floor to climb the stairs to the kitchen telephone and attempt to track him down.

My foot had just hit the bottom step of the stairs when the telephone rang. I climbed the stairs, answered the phone and heard a voice on the other end say, "Karl, this is Billy Gray, calling from the Methodist Church. The men here have decided they'd like to do more to help out in support of the Scout troops and asked me to contact you to find what you think we could do to help!"

Oh, what joy to find yourself in the midst of God's will! How majestic and wonderful He is! How utterly beyond understanding are His ways! But to be in the midst of His will and experience meeting Him in the time and place of His design is beyond any description! After nearly 17 months of struggle for me to get completely resolved regarding what God wanted me to do, God met me in the same minute coming the other way!

I poured out my heart to Billy and told him it was essential that I get to the men's club as soon as possible to present my apology. He answered that their regular monthly meeting was the following night. Could I come?

Wild horses could not have kept me away.

18

An Adventure in Forgiveness — Part III

"See to it that no one comes short of the grace of God; that no root of bitterness springing up causes trouble, and by it many be defiled."
Hebrews 12:15

I didn't know what to expect when I arrived at the Methodist Men's Club meeting. Billy Gray had me placed on the agenda, but I had no idea how the meeting would be conducted or when I would be given opportunity to speak. I was also somewhat nervous, but the Lord gave me an immediate lift in that the president of the group, John, evidenced the Holy Spirit in all his efforts. John's opening prayer and gentle and persuasive control of the meeting were a great encouragement. There were fifteen men present.

As the meeting progressed, it became evident that I was going to be the last item on the agenda, and it was quite a long list of items that were being covered. I had plenty of time to think about what I was going to say and how I was going to say it. I carefully rehearsed the topics and even the words, just as the prodigal son had (Luke 15:18-19), especially the exact words with which I would seek to receive forgiveness by the men. As I was doing this, the Lord interrupted me and said, "Karl, when you ask to be forgiven, you must receive it from each man individually. Go across the room from left to right from man to man and ask each to forgive you. Do not go on until each has forgiven you." I incorporated this into my plans and waited my turn.

Finally, several hours into the meeting, the opportunity came. I took perhaps thirty minutes to review the background of my earlier years with the Scout troop, the ugly letter, my conversion to Christ, the saga of my search for God's visible presence in the ministry of the Scout troop I was serving and how I had come under conviction of my need for forgiveness for the letter. Then I went across the room, from left to right, asking each man in turn to forgive me. Each of them said,"I forgive you." I thanked them and the meeting closed in prayer shortly thereafter. The men arose from their seats and several approached me, one ahead of the others.

The one who arrived first said, "You'll never know how much your apology means to me. I was president of this men's club when that letter came. I've had two sons who were Scouts, but I became so angry and bitter when I got that letter that I swore I would have nothing to do with Scouting again and I've been actively working ever since against our continuation of any support for these two troops." He began to get louder and more angry, then grabbed the lapels of my jacket in his fists as he continued to increase his expressions of anger and bitterness. John and several other men intervened and pulled him away, pointing out to him that he had just forgiven me in their presence and that the account was now closed. He started to continue his tirade, but again they interrupted and admonished him clearly that it was not appropriate to continue such discussion on a matter on which every individual had agreed was closed forever. He agreed and the matter came to rest. A feeling of complete peace seemed to pervade the entire room. And the wisdom of God in requiring me to obtain from each man his verbal expression of forgiveness in the presence of the others was amply demonstrated.

I left the meeting that night knowing I had been obedient and wondering how I would see the glory of God manifested in the Scout troop.

A few nights later I received a telephone call at home. The caller identified herself as a special education teacher from a nearby school. She explained that they had a particular problem child who had severe learning disabilities and social maladjustment problems, reading at the second grade level and being raised by his grandparents because of the severe drug and criminal problems of his parents. She said that she had inquired of several in the Scouting program and that my name and troop had come up as a potential means of helping this boy, Larry. "Would you be willing to take him into your troop and try to help him?"

I was in tears by the time I hung up the phone. I had not been particularly active in the district Scouting activities, nor had I particularly strong relations with any of the other Scouters in the area. There was certainly no reputation or reason as to why our Scout troop should have been selected for this phone call except that angels of God had directed it. I knew the gates of heaven had been swung open! God was now in our midst! I entered into this new task with all the enthusiasm imaginable.

19

Larry

"But many who are first will be last; and the last, first."
Matthew 19:30

    The week following the special education teacher's phone call, I met Larry. He was brought into the Scout meeting by his grandparents and was everything the teacher had said. He was terribly shy and had difficulty both in learning and forming relationships with other boys. He had the behavior patterns of a much younger boy and tended to stand off from the others, possibly being unsure of himself and expressing himself in ways that quickly alienated him from the other boys. I made special effort to give him help and encouragement and had my hands full in attempting to persuade the other Scouts to open up and make room for him in their activities, despite the difficulties he created.
    He could read at only a second grade level. Hence, though Larry was motivated to learn, he could not make much out of the Boy Scout Handbook, which contained most of the material related to Scouting and its basic skills development. So I undertook to help teach him to read.
    I had him come over to my house on Sunday afternoons, bringing his school reader with him, and we spent an hour or two reading, both out of the Bible and out of his reader. We would identify words he was having difficulty with and write them down separately to take home and learn. Soon I discovered other severe difficulties he was having in math and began to tutor him there, also. This was no doubt one of the most frustrating efforts I have ever undertaken and my shortcomings frequently reduced me to frustrations of anger in which I finally learned to first apologize to Larry and then pray together. Gradually, I began to learn to present math concepts to him in various analogies where he began to capture the ideas, and his progress became much more rapid. We also developed a solid relationship of mutual respect. We became faithful to a difficult task that demanded more of us than we had originally committed to or expected.
    As the year progressed, Larry and his grandparents both reported that his school work had begun to improve dramatically. It was only a little more than a year later that Larry announced to me that he had decided to go to his teacher and state that he felt he had progressed far enough to be taken out of special education classes and put into the regular classroom. I

discounted his report, but was pleasantly surprised a few weeks later when he told me that the request had been approved. His academics continued to improve and within another year or two he was getting a liberal assortment of A's and B's on his report cards.

Things did not progress quite as rapidly in Scouting, but there was significant progress there also. It took Larry a year and a half to make second class Scout and another two years to make first class. By then he had picked up a number of skills and grown in physical coordination and strength. He was usually the first and most successful Scout in getting a campfire going and he took pains to see that younger boys learned the same lessons he had regarding the "right" way to get the job done in the camp or on the trail. For his first four years in Scouting, Larry was repeatedly the Scout who won annual honors for being the most faithful boy in the troop in participation in troop activities and, as I recall, did not miss a single campout during that entire period. He became a near-perfect example of faithfulness, seldom found in either a boy or a man. He seemed to draw a considerable portion of his own life from the Scout troop and he put his life into it, as well. His faithfulness paid off. Shortly after his 16th birthday, he was a Star Scout. By age 17 he was rapidly closing in on Life Scout and intent upon making Eagle.

In the meantime, he had begun to grow in other school activities. He became a member of his school chorus, which later went on to win major regional competitions, and made his high school wrestling team. By the time he was a senior in high school, he was a solid achiever in a variety of areas and was a respected member of both his school and Scout troop.

Larry did successfully complete his Eagle Scout requirements within the time allowed by his 18th birthday. The completed package containing his Scouting record, Eagle Project Report, reference letters and recommendation by the District Eagle Board of Review were forwarded to national headquarters for approval and shortly thereafter it was my pleasure as Scoutmaster to present him with his Eagle Award at a special Eagle Scout Court of Honor.

This story has been recounted numerous times. It is both a testimony of God's love and power to work in the lives of those who are obedient to Him and a vivid example of the power of Boy Scouting in the life of a boy.

**Scouts Approaching Lakes-of-the-Clouds
AMC Hut, White Mountains, New Hampshire — 1965**

**New Scouts Approaching an Expanded
Hut, High Adventure — 1980**

20

Parade Ground Miracle

"For I, too, am a man under authority, with soldiers under me; and I say to this one, 'Go!' and he goes, and to another, 'Come!' and he comes, and to my slave, 'Do this!' and he does it."

Matthew 8:9

    The bugle sounded over the evening parade ground. As the color guard began to lower the colors, an unusual stillness fell on the hundreds of observing Scouts. An anointing of the Holy Spirit fell over my head and shoulders, witnessing to me that something very special was happening that was of the Lord. This was not merely an evening colors ceremony. It was not even the special ceremony for which I had prepared my Scouts. It was something more.

    The place was Camp Olmstead at the Goshen Scout Camp, home of the four major Scout summer camps for the National Capital Area Council, of the greater Washington, D.C. area. The year was 1980 and I had taken troop 659 to Camp Olmstead for the second year in a row after reassuming the Scoutmastership in 1978. The preceding year had left me somewhat concerned over the lack of spirit and Scout tradition in the camp, including lack of any morning and evening colors. So, when the camp director greeted us upon arrival with an invitation to help out in any way that we might desire, I leapt at the chance to provide an evening colors ceremony on one of the upcoming evenings. I selected Wednesday night.

    One of the first tasks was to find a bugler. Colors without a bugler are not really colors, and our troop had none. So we searched all the different troop sites and found a Scout troop with a bugler. (Actually, we found two and held an audition, selecting the best one!) Then we had to select four boys for a color guard. I selected two older and two younger Scouts who I thought would be able to reliably learn the military procedures for proper conduct of a color guard ceremony. We started to work.

    First, I reviewed with them how to perform a proper military "left-face" and "right-face." Then I taught them how to commence marching and halting together, with the boy in the rear quietly calling the commands and cadence so that only the other three Scouts could hear (but not observers). They practiced "about face", then stepping forward together to retrieve the flag and properly fold it. We practiced around our troop camp, then went out on the parade ground and practiced with a flag and the flag pole we were to use. We included the bugler on our last rehearsal and taught him the procedures for him to "sound off." We intended to set an example to the whole camp on what an evening colors ceremony could be.

Wednesday night arrived and all the Scouts of the camp took their places in front of the dining hall. An announcement was made that we would observe evening colors and we all turned to face the flag pole. I took a place where I could view the whole proceedings and take some photos.

From the edge of the field came our color guard. Walking precisely in step they came across the parade ground to the flag pole, all wearing full uniform, heads straight ahead and the very example of Scouting's finest appearance. As if by magic they halted exactly even with the flag pole, their feet stopping together in unison as if they were a precision military drill team. This was amazing! There was not a flaw of any kind in their execution! Even the U.S. Marines could not surpass this! Then, with the same precision, they made a right face together to face the flag. The two center Scouts simultaneously took one step forward to prepare to retrieve the colors. The head of the color guard ordered, "Bugler, sound off!"

This was the moment when the special hush and anointing of God fell on the camp. The sound of the bugle call carried through the quiet air. The beauty of our red, white and blue flag reflected in the sunlight as it slowly, solemnly descended, signifying the close of day. A tremendous sense of awe in the majesty of our flag seemed to hang in the air, all that it stands for and the inspiration of those who established our nation. Tears started down my cheeks. The two center Scouts took the flag, folded it and, as if operating from the same mind, simultaneously stepped back to rejoin the other two. Then, continuing with the same precision with which they had come on the field, they made a crisp right face and began marching off the parade field. The hush continued for a few more moments, then the camp staff director began the evening meal routine and the spell was broken.

I exulted and wondered at the magic of the moment.

What had happened? Why had things gone so flawlessly? Surely, despite rehearsal, something always goes wrong during actual execution, does it not? Why had God chosen to so lavishly grace our conduct of an evening colors ceremony? Scoutmasters of other troops began to come up to me during and after dinner to congratulate me, several saying it was the best color guard ceremony they had ever seen in their lives!

I continued to exult and think about the magnificence of the ceremony while preparing to check out of camp. I had arranged for a split week with one of the Scout's fathers and planned to head home Thursday morning. That morning I took my check-out sheet to the Camp Director's office. We chatted for a few moments before he brought up the subject.

"That sure was a good flag ceremony you guys did last night!"

"Thanks very much!"

"We couldn't have picked a better night to have it!"
"Really?"
"Yes! Do you know who that man was who was with me last night?"
"No! I didn't realize you had somebody with you."
"We had a special guest, General Olmstead, the retired Army general for whom this camp is named."
"No kidding!
"Yes! This is the first visit he has ever made to the camp since it was named for him seven or eight years ago! And when were walking around camp earlier in the day, one of the things he asked me was whether we held evening colors ceremonies."
"Wow!"
"I told him, 'Yes we did' ...But that's the first one we've had in a long time."
"That's incredible."
"He said that was the best evening colors ceremony he's ever seen!"

21

ADD 659

> *"...before they call, I will answer; and while they are still speaking, I will hear."*
>
> Isaiah 65:24

We knew we needed a truck. Not just for Scouting. My wife and I had talked for months of our need to haul firewood for our household and hay for her horse as well as Boy Scout equipment for the Scout troop. Now it seemed it was about time we started looking. It was February. If we started now, we could be in a position to know what we wanted by June.

After a few visits to used car places, it seem that the urgency increased to go ahead and buy a truck now, without waiting until June. Prayer seemed to confirm this, so we decided to proceed. We had seen several trucks that we liked, but didn't know which we liked best. While looking at one of them a few days later, we suddenly felt impressed to go out to our car and pray over the matter. We told the salesman what we were going to do and excused ourselves.

Getting into our car, we began praying, "Lord, You are the One who has given us the desire and ability to buy a truck. This truck and its purposes are Yours. We desire to know which truck You want us to buy and how much of the money You have placed in our care You want us to pay for it. It is Your money and Your truck, Lord. Thank You for hearing us and answering this request. In Jesus' name, Amen."

Returning to the salesman, we began to inquire of him further regarding the truck in which we were interested and discovered quickly that his ideas and ours regarding possibilities on a deal were miles apart. We departed, rejoicing that God had apparently eliminated at least that possibility from the list.

The following evening I had planned to revisit another truck we admired a few days earlier, but earlier in the afternoon I had an appointment with my pastor, Bill Denston. Meeting in his office, we had a long chat over several subjects and somewhat lost track of time. After nearly two hours of discussion, his phone suddenly rang and he answered it. It was his wife, inquiring when he would be coming home for dinner. Before he had a chance to turn to me for an estimate of the time, the line was interrupted by another call. It was my wife, with the identical question for me. It was such an unusual and precise coincidence of calls that it caught my attention. We quickly told our wives we were breaking up our meeting immediately and would come straight home.

As I got into my car and started the engine, I was suddenly flooded with the knowledge that I was perfectly within the will of God at exactly the time and place He wanted me, for some mysterious purpose. He impressed upon me that there was a divine perfection in my position in His will even as to the exact position of my car as I drove out onto Franconia Road and headed for home. This particular thought overwhelmed me even as it raised the question in my mind, "Why would God want to impress upon me that I am in the particular time and place that He wants me?" I drove up to the stop light at Telegraph Road and stopped, the first car at the light.

As the light turned green I turned right and was astonished to see driving along directly in front of me the identical truck that I was planning to revisit in another hour. I thought for a moment that the truck must have been sold and I was following the new owner! But then I seemed to realize in a flash that God was confirming for me that this was the model truck that I was to buy. As my astonishment increased, the truck now suddenly turned left onto my own side street! Was this truck now to lead me into the driveway of my own house? In another few moments I realized that the truck undoubtedly belonged to a neighbor; that if I continued to follow it, I would probably be able to inquire of him as to his experience with it, any problems he might have had, and how much he had paid for it. So I followed until he came to a halt in front of a house a few blocks from mine.

I hopped out and introduced myself and my purpose. The truck owner was quite generous in giving me answers to all my questions. I received a first hand consumer's report. He was highly satisfied with his truck and had paid much less for his than I had been prepared to offer. I went home and excitedly told my wife of what had happened. She confessed that that model had been her favorite all along.

After dinner I returned to the auto dealer to find the truck of our choice still on the lot. I test drove it one more time and made an offer on it $2000 less than the listed price. The salesman seemed somewhat surprised that the manager accepted it and asked me how I had arrived at that particular offer. I explained the whole story to him and told him that I thought God had shown me how much I was to pay for the vehicle He told me to buy. We closed the deal and I thought that was the end of the affair.

But we still had to register the vehicle. It was the first truck we had owned and the first vehicle we had registered in the State of Virginia. We went through the routine of sending in the title and awaiting our new registration tags.

When the license plates arrived, we were astonished. The plates read, "ADD 659."

"659" was the number of my Boy Scout troop, and I was the Scoutmaster!

22

Helping Hands

"...before they call, I will answer..."
Isaiah 65:24

It was fall, 1983. The Scout troop was operating well, except for one thing: There was a persistent lack of adult support, particularly male adult participation in the campouts and the supervision of troop meetings. This problem, so typical of most youth programs, seemed to be growing for our Scout troop. As mentioned in other chapters, many of the families in the troop had no fathers and those we had seemed resistant to participating. Others were leaving because their sons were leaving Scouting. As autumn progressed, the number of active men shrank to just two or three — not enough to run a troop effectively. There remained only two men regularly supporting the weekly meetings and campouts, Assistant Scoutmaster Dick Siler and me. Since two adults were required for nearly all activities, it meant that we had to participate in all events. No flexibility was available for the demands of our professions, families or contingencies.

I'd been noticing these problems for some time and had been praying about it. While asking God for more men, I was also wondering if the troop had somehow fallen out from under God's blessing or if, perhaps, God was signalling me not to presume that He would always retain His blessing on the Scout troop as a ministry. I even considered the possibility that removal of such key resources as the men might be an indication that God was now planning to discontinue the troop. I continued to pray about it.

One night Dick brought up the subject in a way that couldn't be ignored, stating frankly that we could not continue to operate without more men to help. I agreed and told him I'd been considering a range of possibilities and felt that we were at a crisis as to whether or not God wanted us to continue the Scout troop. We both agreed that if the troop were to continue, God would have to provide additional help.

I suggested we pray together. At the back of the meeting hall we bowed our heads and prayed out loud that if God intended that we continue as a Scout troop, He would have to provide us with additional help and that He would show us the direction He desired us to go by how He answered the prayer. We then continued the activities of the troop meeting.

Some years later, Dick was recalling the incident in a letter. He said, "Do you remember the time when all our help had dropped out or moved on or something and we needed someone badly in Troop 659? I remember that you suggested that we have prayer and ask the Lord if he wanted us to continue as a troop. There weren't any lightning bolts or immediate answer, but about 20 minutes later, in walked a young man, age 24, in an Eagle (Scout) uniform, named Ron Prettyman. He said that he was new to the area, owed a lot to Scouting, and was looking for a troop that needed some help."!

God's answer to that prayer was far more than a mere "walk-on." Ron was a wonderfully gifted young man who set immediately to work with the troop, continuing full time until he moved from the area some years later. Faithful, gifted in teaching and wonderfully competent in Scouting, he set a model example of patience and availability to the Scouts. He introduced new ideas into the troop's advancement program and by his creative genius (as an electrical engineer) made subjects of applied science into demonstrations to which teenage boys could relate. He became a very special blessing to the troop, both to the boys and the adults.

There was also something special in the manner in which the Lord answered this particular need after previous individual prayer had been left unanswered. By bringing our legitimate need out into the open as He did, and obliging our public prayer for a definitive answer, God increased His glory among us. He challenged our faith and then proved His Headship in a manner which private prayers would not have accomplished. It gave all of us definitive direction and did a work in each of our hearts to increase our faith in God. As Dick put it years later, referring to the moment Ron walked in and announced his purpose, "Well, that was enough for me. I will never forget that experience!"

23

Scoutmaster's Son

"He said to Me, 'Thou art My Son, Today I have begotten Thee. Ask of Me, and I will surely give the nations as Thine inheritance, and the very ends of the earth as Thy possession.'"

Psalm 2:7,8

"Dad, I'd like to quit Scouts." The voice of my son came to me from the back seat of the car as he, his mother and I were driving down the road. I knew he had arranged to speak with me at a time when Gretchen was present, and I had been expecting to hear this for some time. The signs had been evident and I had wondered how I would reply when his decision came to quit Scouts.

Kenny was 15 years old and a Star Scout. He was one merit badge away from Life Scout and had just been elected Senior Patrol Leader. He was an outstanding leader, having a special knack for getting along well with nearly all types of adults and boys, as well as having a formidable set of Scouting skills which enabled him to do easily tasks with which many struggled. He had been on every High Adventure Trip with the Scout troop since he was 10 years old. He wasn't afraid of getting his hands dirty to see that a job got done right. But he was a procrastinator and working on advancement did not come easily to him.

In addition, the sons of Scoutmasters have a special tribulation in their dealings with both other Scouts and their fathers. To a certain extent, the other Scouts think that the Scoutmaster's son has some sort of special privilege or "gets away" with things that the other boys can't, when actually, of course, the opposite is true. The Scoutmaster, being unable to treat his own son exactly as the other Scouts, always makes sure that he will err on the side of tighter standards and scrutiny of his son. In addition, whenever a volunteer is needed to buy food, work out a logistics action with the quartermaster, remember to bring something, or otherwise "fill in the gap," that Scout can't escape the convenience of being nearly under the Scoutmaster's very nose when the need is discovered. In the son's perceptions, all these factors are magnified to decrease Scouting's pleasures for him.

Also, there is the burden of obligation which seems to be implied by being the son of the Scoutmaster. Isn't it implied that he is in for the duration of his Scouting career? Isn't it assumed that he will go on to attain the rank of Eagle Scout? Don't his standards of faithfulness have to match his father's? Will he make his father feel bad or look bad if he decides he has had enough of Scouting? He gets into the performance trap, where he may think he has to perform certain duties to Scouting to make his father happy with him (or even, possibly, to earn his approval).

Like the smell of campfire smoke, the scent of Kenny's spirit had filled the air around him for several months. I had reviewed it all in my mind before Kenny ever broached the subject and had prepared to free him from any bondage or guilt feelings. To do this, I had first had to free my own spirit. I had settled in my heart that Kenny was neither in Scouting to satisfy my ambitions nor to earn anything with me. I was sorry that he wanted to leave, but he would have to make the decision himself in preparation for other life decisions he was soon to confront as a young man. He would not be the first Scout to drop out. Life would go on.

Nevertheless, when his statement came from the backseat, I was not prepared for a specific answer. I thought about it for about a half minute or so, and asked the Lord how I should answer. He answered me with three conditions and the words came naturally.

"Okay, you can drop out of Scouting ... only there are three things you must do first."

An audible sigh of relief came out of the backseat as my son said, "Great, what are they?"

"First, you were just elected Senior Patrol Leader three weeks ago. You accepted the job and were elected in good faith by the Scouts. You must finish the normal minimum of six months on the job for the troop. Second, you have one more merit badge to complete for Life Scout. Pick a merit badge and finish it so you can leave Scouting as a Life Scout."

Kenny readily accepted both of these. They had a kind of "ring" to them that gave them credibility. I was not so sure how the third condition would go over with Kenny.

"Third, I want you to find one Scout activity outside our Scout troop where you can participate in some other service to Scouting with other Scouts. Pick some event such as Junior Leader Training and serve on the staff, or something similar to that which will give you a personal experience of Scouting outside the troop."

Kenny seemed most pleased. He had his ticket to freedom and the conditions seemed fair. It was done with. The issue was closed.

The issue hardly came up again. Kenny finished a weekend on the District staff working with Junior Leader Training and cruised through the winter and spring continuing as Senior Patrol Leader, doing a good job. When he made Life Scout, I presumed he would soon be on his way. But by the fall of 1986, Larry (the Scout described in an earlier chapter) had completed his requirements for Eagle Scout. I am not sure why Kenny was still in Scouting when the time for Larry's Eagle Court of Honor came around.

There is something special about an Eagle Scout Court of Honor. Prestige, recognition of years of hard work and fun, personal appreciation by parents, leaders and distinguished speakers, the review of growth and accomplishments by the Scout, sometimes even recognition accorded by national leaders, (occasionally including the President of the United States) are all part of it. Woven into all this is the spirit of Scouting — the tangible fruit of holding to ideals, of being faithful and loyal until the goal is reached. It is another mystery as to how this reaches the heart of a man. But it has a powerful effect.

Kenny turned to his mother during the proceedings and said, "I'm going for it."

That set the stage for another round of learning for me as Scoutmaster. I knew the difficulties of assisting Scouts over their personal hurdles in planning and executing Eagle Projects and completion of merit badges. Their weaknesses at planning are legend. But each boy usually has other weaknesses, as well, which will step in the way to impede him if he is not provided the proper help. I had to give Kenny his help while leaving the door open for him to quit, if he wanted to. I had to be involved and committed to help him succeed, while allowing him the room to fail, if that was where his decisions led him. Kenny's problem was still procrastination.

He horsed around for six months or so, finally getting an Eagle Project approved. He then failed to keep several commitments in showing up at the National Park office where his project supervisor worked. After the third or fourth time, he received a letter in the mail advising him that due to his lack of faithfulness, his project was cancelled. It caused grief to the Scoutmaster, but joy to the father! Here was an independent and objective source of authority speaking into my son's life regarding his weakest area. Was he listening? Would he rise to the occasion and surmount the greater obstacle he now had to overcome — starting from scratch to put together another Eagle Project?

Inch by inch, he did it, while the ghost of procrastination stalked Kenny. Now we went into the winter months. Everything got harder. "As you sow, so you shall reap." Postponements for rain resulted in new dates where the temperature was well below freezing. Holes had to be dug in frozen soil! Boys didn't show up. Then getting the approvals, the correspondence, the certifications, and so on all proved immensely difficult. It seemed as though God purposefully brought Kenny up against one man after another who procrastinated, failed to keep his word or seemed to lose things! Then the guidance on Eagle Project Reports was changed. Kenny had to do his report over! It was an interesting lesson for a father and Scoutmaster attempting to assist, observe, teach and pray all at the same time, wondering how it all would come out.

It came out that Kenny did earn his Eagle and had his own Eagle Scout Court of Honor shortly before the troop went to California for its 1988 High Adventure Trip. What a proud moment it was for him — the glory of victory, the satisfaction of accomplishing something worthwhile and finishing his Scouting as a boy with something that all will recognize in the future as the mark of a special person — an Eagle Scout.

He is the third generation in his family to achieve the rank. But his father knows very well that the key decision he made in assisting his son was that he first let go. It was the son's decision and direction that determined the outcome.

Kenny was quite forthright in preparing for his trip to California. "When we get on the airplane, I'm going to go back and forth to the bathroom every hour or so, so that everyone on that plane can see that I'm an *Eagle Scout!*"

**Fishing the High Sierras, Lake Wallace
Sequoia National Park High Adventure — 1988**

The Reward

24

Patterns of Providence

"I have aroused him in righteousness, and I will make all his ways smooth."
Isaiah 45:13

The date was August 11, 1985. Scout Troop 659 had just finished its annual High Adventure trip to the White Mountains of New Hampshire and we were visiting the U.S.S. Constitution ("Old Ironsides") in the Boston Navy Yard on our way home to Alexandria. We had thoroughly explored the oldest ship in the United States Navy and had decided that we could afford to take the Scouts to the Maritime Museum on the opposite side of the Navy Yard pier. The cost of the museum was $2.50, according to the historic guide brochure, but it seemed worthwhile so we gathered our troop and headed over to the museum. At the front door, the sign read as follows: "100 years ago today, the U.S.S. Constitution ("Old Ironsides") visited Alexandria, Virginia and Washington, D.C. All visitors who are residents of those cities may visit the museum today free of charge."

Almost from the beginning of scheduling High Adventure Trips for Scout Troop 659, there began to be evidenced unusual degrees of divine providence. I didn't notice the pattern for several years and so think I have forgotten a few of the many incidents. They reflect the royal personality and sense of humor of Jesus Christ as well as His character-building purposes and power.

The first incident I clearly recall was in August, 1979 on the first of Troop 659's High Adventure Trips. We were over 6000 feet high on the north ridge of Mt. Mitchell, North Carolina, the tallest mountain in the eastern United States, having just hiked four miles and climbed 2,500 feet to reach Deep Gap Shelter. I was all set to lead an exploration of the ridge, which was covered with alpine meadows, evergreen trees and other alpine flora, when I discovered that I had left my movie film in the car at the bottom of the mountain! We had three more days on the mountain, including the trip over the summit of Mt. Mitchell, and I had kept a tradition for years of recording the High Adventure Trips (and only the High Adventure Trips) on 8mm. movies. I was crushed at the thought of not being able to record this part of our trip, but the notion did not seriously enter my mind to walk back to the foot of the mountain and fetch the movie film, a round trip of eight miles!

Then the two oldest boys, both Life Scouts, said, "Mr. Duff, what will you give us if we go back down and get the movie film for you?"

I looked at Mike and Paul in astonishment. Both were strong, experienced boys and, travelling together without packs, I did not see any difficulty in their going as a pair. After a few minutes of negotiation and consideration, I discovered that they were quite content with Big Mac's and milkshakes when we got back to civilization, a price I was more than willing to pay. So off they went, with appropriate emergency items of clothing and equipment with them. They returned from the eight mile, 5000 vertical feet trip in less than three hours, a remarkable display of strength and conditioning even among older Scouts.

The reader might not consider this to be so much an incident of divine providence as a provision wrought out of resources at hand. I would agree, except for the extreme degree of gratitude I felt at provision being made to cover one of my mistakes, which was totally beyond me to accomplish myself, and which was furthermore beyond anything I would have thought of asking another person to do. However, to make the point that the Lord was with us, He gave us another incident on the way home.

On the last day of our trip, we exited the mountains and started our drive home. On the way, I got some grit in my eyes and severely scratched them. I wear contact lenses, but found myself unable to keep them in because of the painful sensitivity of my eyes. The next morning, they were even more sensitized and I was faced with the prospect of having to drive for seven hours from North Carolina to Washington, D.C. with uncorrected vision.

I searched for alternatives but could find none. The other adult on the trip had to drive his own car. I prayed that God would keep us safe en route. We had not travelled very far down the road when I noticed my vision improving. Within an hour or so I was seeing 20/20, easily reading all the road signs and license plates. After we safely returned home, my eyes reverted to their normal uncorrected vision of 20/120.

In 1980, we went to New Hampshire's White Mountains and planned two successive four-day "loop" trips, between which we restocked with food from the large moving van in which we traveled. In addition, we had planned to rendezvous with the father of one of the boys who was supposed to drive up from Washington to meet us for the second half of the trip. Jerry had a bit of a reputation for unreliability and did not show up for the rendezvous. Knowing that he could possibly show up late, but unwilling to hold up the trip on that remote chance, I decided to drive to the nearest telephone some five or ten miles away at the Appalachian Mountain Club (AMC) Hostel in Crawford Notch to attempt to phone him or leave a message. Failing to reach him, I was in the process of writing a short note to leave with the manager of the hostel, when the same phone I'd just used rang. The manager of the hostel answered it, turned to me and asked if I were Karl Duff. The caller was Jerry, who was still in Washington but who had attempted to reach the U.S. Forest Service and had been advised to try leaving a note for me at the hostel! By the three or four minute margin of time that I had been at the hostel and remained to scratch out that short note, we made contact with each other.

Jerry had been calling to cancel, but as a result of this stroke of providence, he was persuaded to drive all night to attempt to reach us. Again, I did not have high confidence that he would actually make it, but it appeared that God was working to facilitate Jerry's making the trip in spite of himself. I gave him instructions on where to meet us and the Scout troop concluded the day by hiking a mile or two into the mountains and setting up the next overnight camp.

The next morning, Jerry had not showed up. While cooking breakfast, I began thinking some more about Jerry's aggravating way of doing things and wondered what I should do. I decided to hike back out to the road, drive again up to the hotel and see if there were any messages. Finding none, I left a note with our itinerary on the truck, which I parked on the side of the road, just in case Jerry should show up and desire to follow us into the mountains. I got back to camp at precisely the time I had told the Scouts to be ready to hike out. They were ready; we had our packs on and were hiking out when up the trail came Jerry! He had found my note just a few moments after I had left it and followed me right up the trail. One minute later and Jerry would have found only an empty campsite after a trip all the way from Washington, D.C.!

Many times we have prayed for rain to stop and have seen the skies clear, or had the best day of the trip occur when we made the major mountain climb of the trip, as in the case of Mt. Katahdin, Maine in 1981. An urge to hunt for blueberries has been rewarded by finding patches the rangers didn't even know about, to vindicate our having carried around an "extra" box of pie dough or bisquick, just in case we would find berries to make a special dessert! The same has been true of our fishing. Usually everyone who brings a fishing pole has caught fish!

In 1983, we went to Rocky Mountain National Park, Colorado and had made careful plans and preparations for our most complex High Adventure Trip ever. Through an error in the computer of one of the airlines, which had failed to clear an extremely low air fare rate after the spring rates went into effect, we obtained round trip air fare to Denver for $198 per person (via Salt Lake City). Ground transportation and careful selection of a camp immediately outside the park boundary for a couple of nights to acclimatize enabled us to maximize the utilization of our seven days allowed within the National Park itself. We carefully planned use of gas stoves in those places it was required, and an itinerary that was perfect for good hiking, fishing and even a trip on a glacier. All went off without a hitch, except for one thing. Despite all my efforts to locate them, I was unable to find commemorative patches of Rocky Mountain National Park at any of the stores we went to, and we were planning to leave the National Park area directly upon pick-up by our ground transportation. I could not go home without patches for each participant! Five days into the trip, I still had not figured out how to solve this problem. However, that evening the boys made friends with two single girls, the first hikers we had seen since the start of our trip, who shared a campsite close to us. They were planning to exit the National Park in an area where there was a souvenir shop. They agreed to buy us the patches and mail them to us! Everything worked out great. Meeting the two girls also gave our wild and wooly Scouts the chance to "fall in love" with the older girls, agree to write letters, and teach the girls how to play their favorite game, "liars' dice"!

For any young ladies who should read this, please take note that both of the above girls, after having taken leave of their boyfriends to travel around the country and go hiking together, received marriage proposals within their first two weeks after returning home. Their absence had helped both boy friends decide that they couldn't live without them. Was this providence also, or is this an instructive strategy to young ladies with undecided boy friends?

One of the most difficult and amazing interventions of God occurred on our 1984 trip to central Canada for a canoeing High Adventure. On the way home, while driving around the north side of Lake Superior in our school bus at 2:30 a.m. on a Sunday morning, the torque converter on the automatic transmission failed. The first car coming the other way stopped to help and was driven by an automobile mechanic! He had just received Jesus Christ as Lord and Savior a few months earlier. He diagnosed the failure, gave us a ride into town to attempt to wake up the right people from a towing company and the local General Motors agency, and stayed with us until we had towed the bus into town and got the troop situated at a nearby provincial park camping ground. Then he headed for points west with his two hitchhikers still in the back seat; they had watched the whole proceedings for nearly eight hours.

Despite the auspicious start, we still had to wait for three days for a replacement torque converter to be shipped out from Toronto. We cooled our heels somewhat impatiently, fishing, swimming, exploring for agates and amethysts and praying for the torque converter to hurry up! On the evening of the third day, while emerging from the restaurant where we had taken the troop for dinner, two of the older Scouts, Kenny and Dan, noticed a Purolator Courier truck parked out front and said, "Say, wasn't it a Purolator truck that was supposed to bring our part out from Toronto?" Realizing that this might be the truck that was delivering the vital part to the General Motors regional parts distributor, located 100 miles further to the west, I went back into the restaurant and found the driver.

"Yes," he said when he checked his shipping list, "I do have such a part for the local agency. However, I could never release the part without it being received and signed for by the local GM dealer." I jumped into the van which the local GM dealer had loaned us for the three days and sped down to their place of business. The last man from the shop was just locking the door and heading home for the night! He returned with me and we found the part, among many hundreds in the back of the huge trailer, in the very first cage we checked!

By that intuitive stroke of recognition by two of our Scouts, we were saved nearly 24 hours in the repair of the bus and were on our way by noon the next day.

During this forced stay in Schreiber, Ontario, we were given free camping, free use of a long-bodied van by the GM dealer and the bus repairs were covered by warrantee. The only financial consequence we experienced was for the extra food.

In 1986 on our High Adventure to the State of Washington, we met two newspapermen from the *Everett Daily Herald* out for a week of hiking and doing a feature story of the Cascade Trail for their newspaper. One was a writer and the other was a photographer. They traveled with us for several days on the trail. Our Scout troop ended up being the feature of a front page color photograph and major article in the *Herald* a few weeks later!

The list would undoubtedly go on if we were not running out of years. In 1987, we went sailing on Chesapeake Bay, using one of the large 45-foot sailing sloops of the U.S. Naval Academy sailing club. On the morning of the second day, we awoke to find that the battery bank was dead and we had no way to start our diesel engine. After a day of incredible unplanned adventure, we succeeded in making our way under sail back into the inner harbor of Annapolis and tying up only five minutes before the small boat naval facility closed for the night! It was just sufficient time for them to designate a new set of batteries for us if we would change them ourselves. While doing this and also trying to figure out how we could identify and correct the problem which had caused the failure, a government vessel from another home port came in behind us to tie up. I asked the skipper if they had an electrician on board and they did. In twenty minutes he had found a faulty voltage regulator wire, repaired it and we were on our way! By sailing under the moon well past midnight, we were able to recover our original schedule and have a wonderful trip. The elements of adventure which challenged us that second day were wonderful things that we would never have designed for ourselves.

God desires to overtake us with His blessings (Deut. 28:2) and performs His signs among us that we may know of His great character and exalt Him as Lord (Ex. 10:2, Ps. 46:10, Ps. 103). Yet how unfathomable are His ways. How can we claim to understand His love and provision for us? As the psalmist David said, "Such knowledge is too wonderful for me. It is too great, I cannot attain to it" (Ps. 139:6).

We are told that we can be His witnesses, telling of the great things He has done (Is. 43:10).

Patterns of Providence 113

**A Tough Passage, Canada Canoe
Trip High Adventure — 1984**

**Trimming the Sails, Chesapeake
Bay High Adventure — 1987**

25

Law of Generations

"The LORD, the LORD God, compassionate and gracious, slow to anger, and abounding in lovingkindness and truth ... yet He will by no means leave the guilty unpunished, visiting the iniquity of fathers on the children and on the grandchildren to the third and fourth generations."
Exodus 34:6,7

Once I recognized my own sin nature and had begun to cooperate with its being put to death through the Lordship of Jesus Christ, I became alert to observe its operation in the Scouts with whom I worked. Its astonishing power to deceive and imprison is demonstrated repeatedly, sometimes under the most unexpected circumstances. In addition, however, the power of God's precepts to deliver were also frequently demonstrated. "...Where sin increased, grace abounded all the more" (Rom. 5:20).

One morning at Scout summer camp, our troop got up early for a special canoe outing of several hours before breakfast, scheduled for boys who were taking the canoeing merit badge class. We launched our canoes and commenced a long paddle across the beautiful waters of Camp Parsons on Hood Canal, Washington. Jim and Russ were together in one canoe and were eager to race, being the strongest pair in the troop. They would periodically come up alongside each of the other canoes and challenge them to a race. Soon they were out near the head of the pack. Though they were strong, their canoeing style was atrocious and I knew that it was not in keeping with the instruction they should be receiving in the merit badge class. I considered myself an expert, and volunteered some instruction regarding their grip of the paddle and a proper stroke which would enable them to keep their canoe going in a straight line without constantly shifting paddles from one side to the other. Picking up on these pointers was not at all conducive to their continuing to demonstrate their canoe racing prowess. They ignored me.

I became irritated at being ignored and admonished them a bit more forcefully, which they also ignored. Early in the discussion I had been primarily interested in the long-term benefits of their learning proper canoeing techniques, but about this stage of the game I became focused on getting them to respond to my authority and doing it my way. I failed to heed the warning signs and continued to admonish them, indicating I was going to take up the issue of proper technique with their class instructor. That brought a strong retort from Jim.

By this time we were all angry. Continuing to paddle along silently, I indignantly thought through my alternatives for obliging them to give some sort of response to my instructions, when the Lord interrupted me. "Why, Karl? The purpose of this morning is to have a good time, not to give instruction. You've been hassling them." I quickly changed my mind about what to do and decided to ask their forgiveness for hassling them when next we came into shore.

About a half hour further down the beach, the trip leader took us all in to the beach for a short rest stop and a light bite to eat before turning around and heading back to the camp. I went up to Jim and Russ and apologized for hassling them and asked them to forgive me. Russ forgave me immediately, but Jim said, "I don't know. I'll think about it." It was clear that he was nurturing the offense and was not eager to let it go. Just before we boarded the canoes again, I approached Jim a second time and asked him if he wanted to forgive me or keep the account open. He again snarled something at me that indicated he would not easily let it go.

One of the marvels associated in asking forgiveness is that it frees the person who has committed the offense and asked to be forgiven, even if the requested forgiveness is not immediately forthcoming. I was as free as a bird all the way back to camp and thought nothing more about the incident. Jim and Russ beat everyone else back to camp and had already returned their canoe to its stowage place when I came ashore. Jim was standing there waiting for me. As I approached, he said, "Mr. Duff, I just can't hold it back anymore. I forgive you." He ran up to me and flung his arms around me. We had a big embrace there on the beach while every bit of rancor and unhappiness just melted away. It was marvellous to see the beautiful grin on Jim's face and to share with him the new freedom that he was now experiencing. Jim came from a broken home and this may have been his first such opportunity to actually experience the tangible power of forgiving an offense against him.

Another demonstrable effect of the power of sin in human nature is that it can deceive one into believing he has made no error, even to the point of totally distorting the facts surrounding an incident that is only a few moments old and observed by a great many witnesses. This once occurred at breakfast in a mess hall where a group of us were dining with great enjoyment on stacks of pancakes and syrup. One of the boys sitting next to me had just helped himself to more pancakes and hollered quite rudely, "Pass the syrup!" I was tempted to correct him by telling him to add the word "Please," but decided (perhaps based on my experience with Jim!) that it was not appropriate to hassle him at the time. However, the other boys ignored his demand and the syrup was not passed. A few moments later he demanded again, "Pass the syrup!" I corrected him and said, "Say, 'Please!' "

In a flash, in a moment so short that it seemed no conscious thought could have possibly entered the boy's mind, he snapped back, "I said 'Please' the first time!"

Although corrected regarding the facts, it was clear from the boy's response that he was fully convinced that he had asked properly the first time and that he felt he was therefore justified in demanding the syrup in the manner he had after the other boys had ignored him. I was shown through this otherwise trivial incident's demonstration how poorly we observe the truth about ourselves when it doesn't agree with how we want to appear in our own eyes or in the eyes of others. More than anything else, it seems we want to want to appear to be righteous, even though we are not willing to behave that way.

On the same trip, two boys later got into an altercation in which something got broken and blows were struck. The two Scouts were separated and a review of the incident undertaken. The Scout who had retaliated the most vigorously, though having a legitimate grievance against the other boy, seemed unable to respond to the question, "What did you do then?" Every form of answer he gave was an accusation against the other boy. We continued to pursue questioning and, even though an acknowledgement of the other boy's offense was made, the second boy seemed to be incapable of making any kind of statement regarding what he himself had done. He was so obsessed with justifying his actions that he was capable of no other statement, despite extended and painstaking questioning as to what actions he had undertaken in response to the other boy and despite the presence of many witnesses. In this case it was not possible to gain in the boy's mind an understanding of the truth of his own actions as a basis for reconciliation or discipline.

"Do two men walk together unless they be agreed?" (Amos 3:3) "If we confess [i.e. "agree on"] our sins, He is faithful and righteous to forgive us our sins and to cleanse us from all unrighteousness" (1 John 1:9). "Repent therefore and return, that your sins may be wiped away, in order that times of refreshing may come..." (Acts 3:19) There is an inherent need for people to agree on the truth in order for healthy relationships to thrive. A leader or a boy who is unable to admit his mistakes will not develop much in relationships with others. It is important to persuade young people of this before they carry an unwillingness to admit fault into adulthood, marriage, employment and the raising of families.

There are also other circumstances which may be at work in situations such as those described above and which further complicate restoration and healing, not as easy to recognize.

Bobby was one of the most pleasant Scouts I had ever worked with. He had a delightful and helpful personality, was bright and talented and had a good, healthy family background. Both his mother and father were active and helpful with the troop, his father serving as committee chairman. Over a period of time, though, I noticed that Bobby had difficulty in accepting his share of responsibility in the altercations which he would get into with other boys. Unlike most boys with whom this issue was identified, it seemed that the problem got worse as Bobby got older, not better. By the time he was about 14, it was difficult to get him to agree to any eye-witness report of incidents which had occurred just moments before for which he was culpable.

On one of our High Adventure Trips to New England, an incident which illustrated the problem took place in front of the entire troop. We had finished packing up from a two-day encampment and were just ready to begin hiking on down the trail, when someone discovered Bobby's bright red poncho left out on the ground. It had a Washington Redskins emblem on it and was unique within our group. Everyone immediately recognized it as his.

The boy who picked it up handed it to Bobby to be packed away. Bobby responded, "That's not my poncho!" The Scouts immediately corrected him and pointed out that, of course, it was his poncho. No one else in the group had one like it. I stood at a distance watching the proceedings while Bobby continued to steadfastly insist that he had packed his poncho away in his pack. The Scouts took turns attempting to persuade him that it was obviously his. Why wouldn't he admit it and just pack it away in his pack? With no apparent motive other than the difficulty of admitting he had made a mistake, Bobby continued to insist that his poncho was in his pack. He was clearly ready to leave his poncho behind rather than admit the possibility it was his.

I let the situation run on for a few minutes, thinking it would resolve itself, but finally decided we needed to get on down the trail. I walked up and said, "Okay, we're going to have a pack inspection for ponchos. Everyone get out his poncho. If anyone is missing his, he gets to carry an extra tent."

Immediately Bobby responded, "Well, I guess it is mine," took the poncho and put it into his pack, confirming as he opened his pack that his poncho was missing.

On the long drive home to Washington, D.C. after the trip, Bobby got into a fight with one of the other boys over a photograph a girl had given them. He got the other boy down on the floor in the back of the van and was choking him. After breaking up the fight I called each of the two boys up to the cab one at a time to discuss their behavior. With Bobby, the conversation went something like this:

"Bobby, what were you doing to John?"
"He had my photograph."

"Okay, but tell me what you were doing to him."
"He wouldn't give the picture back to me."
"I understand what he did. Now tell me what you did to him."
"It was my picture and he wouldn't give it back."
"Bobby. I want to hear nothing more from you about what John did. Please tell me what your actions were against him. What were you doing to him when we broke up the fight?"
"He had my picture."

It was the same situation I had seen before, but recurring in Bobby to an extreme degree. Despite repeated attempts to get some kind of basis for agreement in correcting his behavior, he refused to produce even a sentence in which he described his actions. It confounded my approaches to behavioral correction. I decided it was time to discuss it with his parents.

My first mistake was that I approached the problem hastily and, rather than wait until a more opportune time to request a meeting with Bobby's father, I mentioned it to him immediately upon our arrival home after the nine-day absence, while we were unloading the van amidst the happy reunion between the Scouts and their families. It placed a cloud over things which hadn't dissipated by the time I arrived at Bobby's for an appointed meeting a week or so later. The meeting did not go well.

As I reviewed the matter with Bobby's dad, I took care to explain that I did not understand what was going on and was submitting information to him to consider and provide guidance, including instruction for me that he thought was appropriate. As I reviewed each incident which I thought illustrated the problem situation, I received explanations that indicated I was seeing the facts incorrectly, that the mistakes were natural, that I was being judgmental or otherwise jumping to conclusions that were incorrect. I had anticipated difficulty due to my earlier mistake of speaking in haste and to the natural response of parents to defend their children. But I was not fully prepared to find myself on trial. I attempted to alleviate concerns regarding my objectivity by repeating my desire to receive guidance and instruction from the father, but seemed powerless to gain any credibility with him regarding a fairly good list of examples that I thought represented a problem in his son's behavior. Finally, with lots of smiles and pleasantries, including telling me what a "good man" I was, I was escorted to the door. A two-hour effort had produced nothing but denials of any problem whatsoever.

It was only after I got in my car and asked God to help me understand what had happened that I believe I received some insight. I had run into an inherited trait; that is, the son had inherited the same trait as existed in his father. Both were "problem deniers"; neither were able to accept the reality of a problem approached in a confrontational manner. At the most, it was only "somebody else's" problem.

God explains in the Bible that He will pass the weaknesses and attitudes of parents on to children (Ex. 34:7, Num. 14:18, Deut. 5:9). Boy Scouting is not designed to deal with family-rooted problems that are being carried along by Scouts. I was naive when I first discovered this and made some of these mistakes in dealing with boys. This particular mistake cost the troop a good Scout and a good committee chairman. The break in fellowship and unhealed spirits that occurred with this incident caused their departure from the Scout troop within a few months, still under the pretense that everything was all right. It was not all right. The boy joined another troop, but dropped out without making Eagle, though he had all the potential attributes.

I remember that I thought I was doing all right with my life until The Lord finally broke through and showed me my sin and need for a Savior. It was only then that I began to see the truth about myself and discover that agreeing to the truth of my mistakes is a necessary way of life. Looking at it from God's perspective, I realize He must receive the brush-off countless times from His children who refuse to admit they have any problems, thereby cutting off many blessings that God desires to give them.

"A man who hardens his neck after much reproof will be suddenly broken beyond remedy" (Prov. 29:1). God can reduce people who won't respond to the truth to a point of desolation where they are forced to reconsider their situations in a new light, exposed to the Word of Truth. But these options are not available to Scoutmasters or youth workers. I do not discern God's less severe tactics for opening our eyes when we deny the truth. Hence, I do not yet know what practical methods might be open to the leaders of boys who exhibit these problems other than to continue to deal patiently with them and approach each situation carefully after seeking wisdom through prayer.

26

Closing Accounts

"Truly I say to you, whatever you shall bind on earth shall be bound in heaven; and whatever you loose on earth shall be loosed in heaven."
Matthew 18:18

Jon was a bright boy from a broken home. He was impetuous and quick to lose his temper, but also eager to excel and a good camper. He was effective in teaching the younger Scouts the things he had learned and sometimes went out of his way to do so. Although his mother had remarried, his step-father did not take a visibly strong hand in providing discipline. Jon was the greatest handful of rebellion I have ever dealt with in over 25 years as an adult Scouter, constantly refusing to respond to the directions of both Scouts and adult leaders except in tirades of anger.

I early recognized Jon as an agent sent by God to teach me patience, discipline my own emotions and find creative and scriptural solutions to his problems. Over a period of time, I felt I had made some progress in my approaches for getting positive behavior out of him, but was also frequently confronted by other angry adults and boys who did not understand why the Scout troop continued to put up with him. I was forced into frequent prayer in seeking answers to his problems, and struggled, often in vain, to get better control over my own attitudes in the situations in which he would confront me. As I invested more in him, I gradually became more and more his defender. In fact, I know that in time my heart came to be squarely on his side and I could truly say that I loved him and purposed the best for him.

Through several years of confrontation, suspensions and meetings with his parents, Jon continued to feed on Scouting, always coming back for more and gradually growing as he gained more self-confidence, obtaining the series of victories so typical of a boy's life in Scouting. He ultimately reached the rank of Life Scout.

One particular day I was visiting his father on some Scouting business and Jon happened to come into his living room and mention a problem he was having with some of the other Scouts, soon falling into one of his typical tirades over how unfairly he was being treated.

Jon always seemed to be taking offense against everyone for their schemes to deprive him of his rights. He turned every situation into one in which he was maliciously being deprived, punished unfairly, or made to look bad. It was perhaps the unusual setting of his living room and the ease with which, even here, he slipped into the same old patterns of paranoia and anger that made me realize what terrible bondage he lived under. Here, right in his own house, far from Scouting activities, it took merely the drop of a hat to rouse him to a frenzy of anger and jealousy against his fellow Scouts and leaders! What terrible slavery to emotions and attitudes! Wasn't there anything that could be done to help him? I began to realize how much more deadly the venom of his emotions was than the charges of which he accused his brother Scouts, even had they been true. I began to yearn earnestly for his deliverance.

The thought only barely crossed my mind of arguing with Jon regarding the motives and intentions of his fellow Scouts. I knew that my opinions would not move his convictions at all.

"Suppose," I thought, "everything you said of the other Scouts were true and that they actually schemed viciously to take away your recognition, or property, or reputation and worked out a plan to make you look bad and feel bad. Wouldn't it be better for you to just take it and decide to pay the price of whatever they've done to you than to dwell in this bitterness?"

I continued to think, "Wouldn't your own health and happiness improve if you were just to accept the consequences, even though it is not rightfully yours to pay? Can't you afford the cost of forgiving it? Think how free you would be! Consider just paying the price and putting it behind you rather than demanding that others pay."

The issue of how to live in freedom suddenly became so clear! All one needed was to pay the accounts for wrongs suffered by others rather than require the perpetrator to do so. It would end the perpetual "passing on" of sin in the world, caused by the defense of our "rights." The issue seemed to get more precise as I realized that the problem with Jon was not to prove that his fellow Scouts hadn't done the things of which he accused them, but rather that he would be better able to forgive if he just assumed the worst about them; i.e., if he assumed the wrongs suffered were deliberate and vicious rather than thoughtless and accidental.

The Word of God began to flood my mind, revealing the power behind some related stories in the Bible; Moses in the wilderness interceding for the people of Israel after they had worshiped a golden calf, taking the position that if God could not spare Israel from the complete destruction that God pronounced, that He should also take Moses' own name out of the Book of Life. Moses had been willing to take the consequences for the sin of a whole nation onto himself, though innocent of the crime and though it meant his own eternal separation from God! What a picture of intercession! How could God refuse a request based on willingness to suffer death on behalf of someone else's sin? Talk about getting in the way! What a picture of the Father's own plan of salvation for the creation, where His Son, Jesus, would take onto Himself the sins of the world, in order that their accounts could be closed and sin swallowed up! Could God refuse Moses, who was reflecting His own plan of salvation back to Him? He could not, and He spared Israel (Exodus 32).

I sat there soaking in these thoughts, talking to Jon while God continued to show me the riches of His provisions for dealing with wrongs suffered. This was a universal principle! All people should have some capacity to be able to accept unjust wrongs unto themselves, but believers in Christ had an unusual advantage. They had Jesus Himself in them, governing their soul and spirit and acting as the ultimate Payer of suffering consequent to sin. He promised to remove their pain. Believers really are only intermediate "bridges" in accepting the consequences of sin onto themselves, hence onto Jesus. People who walk in this manner are extensions of Christ, placing on Him the sins of the world (much like suction tubes on a vacuum cleaner!). These were the electrifying pictures I had as I felt God illuminate them to me. How could they be applied?

Following some more conversation, I asked Jon if he would like to be free of the bitterness that seemed to control him and tried to illustrate to him how he could put this matter to rest. I encouraged him to decide to accept what he thought these other Scouts had done to him, pay the price and forgive them for it, closing the account forever. After awhile he agreed and we prayed together. I cannot say that there were any earth-shaking events that took place at that moment, but it is possible that there were seeds planted on the principle of forgiveness that will ultimately bear fruit.

The stupendous thing is what happened to me!

Over the next two or three days I excitedly went around sharing the vivid pictures and explanations which I thought God had given me during my conversation with Jon. A couple of evenings later I was recounting these events and principles to some people after a Bible study when suddenly a clarity on the subject that illuminated the righteousness and wisdom of God fell on all of us. It was very powerful. As we began to praise God, there also came a precise realization, a word of knowledge from the Lord (1 Cor. 12:8): "Whenever there is this type of illumination of God's Word, it means that one of us will get an immediate opportunity to apply it; to be put to a test of obedience to walk in it!" There were three of us speaking together at the moment. We departed wondering which of the three would be given a special opportunity to apply these principles.

At this point it is important to describe a separate incident that had taken place the preceding evening between my wife and me. As an amateur horticulturist, I had for many years attempted to transplant many plants and trees from all over the United States to our home in Virginia. One plant with which I had had great lack of success was salal, an evergreen ground shrub from the Pacific Northwest. Only the preceding afternoon I had discovered that, after four or five years of successive failures, one of the most recent plants, which had appeared to have died, had put out a tiny green leaf. Excitedly, I had put a small stick in the ground next to it and taken my wife, Gretchen, out to show it to her, also warning her to beware mistakenly pulling it up as a weed, inasmuch as in its infant state it looked very much like many volunteer trees and weeds that we constantly pull out of our gardens. She assured me that she would be careful not to touch it.

When I came in the following evening after the Bible study, the first thing Gretchen said to me was, "Sit down! I have some bad news for you."

I sat down at the kitchen table.

"I accidently pulled up your salal plant!"

The reader will just have to imagine the cosmic crash that took place at that instant as two universes collided. I was almost ripped apart in the consternation and emotions which followed.

I thought, "How could you? What more painstaking precautions could I have possibly taken to protect the plant from precisely that possibility? It was as though I had had a premonition and was warned to do everything I could to avoid the mistake! What more could I have done? How could you have made such a colossal blunder?"

At the same time I was also thinking, "Wow! How faithful and powerful God is! What a sense of humor! Imagine framing such a situation that would reach into my gizzard like this in such a wonderfully personal way to precisely expose an issue that lays in the very foundation of my personality and interests; that would require me to make a right decision in the treatment of my wife regardless of my longstanding efforts to successfully raise this plant." Not only that, God had faithfully set me up with a knowledge of the answer on how to deal with this lesson and had also warned that "one of the three of us" would have the imminent opportunity to apply the lesson!

Then the surge of emotion came crashing down. "How could she have been so stupid!" "What more could I possibly have done?" and, again, the powerful contervailing realization that God had framed the whole situation for me to exercise, or to refuse to exercise, His precepts of forgiveness.

I struggled in silence for five or ten seconds, looking at Gretchen while inside me the storm raged. I could follow one line or the other. I could rail at my wife with words that were split seconds from my lips, urging me to injure her and hold her accountable, or I could accept the loss and count it as forever paid for out of my own life. I could "swallow up" the mistake or keep it alive and reflect it back onto Gretchen to make her pay. I gathered myself, marvelling at the Lord's beauty, and resolved that the matter was ended forever.

I said, "Well, okay. That's fine. Don't worry about it." We began to talk about other things. This is where the miracle happened.

Gretchen and I sat at the kitchen table talking together for an hour and a half. It was one of the most interesting, stimulating conversations we had ever had, covering many subjects. We lost track of time completely. I never had a thought about the salal plant or the incident. It was not until we got up from the table that I realized what had happened.

God had demonstrated for me His power to cleanse my thoughts and emotions in the action I had taken to bear the cost of accepting my wife's mistake. He had totally dissolved not only my emotions, but even my recollection of the incident. I had been washed through with cleansing, totally consistent with a situation being made of "no account." It was supernatural! The matter had been rendered from a hurricane to a whisper! By having decided I could do as He commanded and bear the cost in my own life, I had opened myself to God's grace and His demonstration of His power to uphold His precepts. What a blessing on our marriage! What a mighty God!

I wish I could I say that, once having had such a mighty demonstration, I have never again railed against my wife. Or that accepting the consequences of other people's mistakes is now second nature to me. I cannot. But I now have a working understanding of the precept of real "close-the-account" forgiveness and a desire to see it more and more at work in my life. And every once in a while I get it right!

This is a discovery that was given me through Scouting. It is my prayer to the Father, in the name of my Creator and Redeemer, Jesus Christ, that it would prove to be as great a blessing in the life of the Scout through whom God revealed it as it has been to me. I also pray that every reader would favorably consider for himself the blessings of applying this precept to his own life, as well as the extreme value of accepting God's forgiveness for his own sins which has been accomplished in the redemptive sacrifice of Jesus Christ.

126 LORD AND SCOUTMASTER

**Mount Washington and Tuckerman
Ravine, White Mountains,
New Hampshire — 1980**

**Mount Katahdin and the Knife
Edge, Baxter State Park, Maine — 1981**

Closing Accounts 127

**The Warning Sign, Approaching
Continental Divide on Mount Flattop,
Rocky Mountain National Park, Colorado — 1983**

"Mountaintop" Experiences While High Adventuring

27

Nature

"The heart is more deceitful than all else and is desperately sick; who can understand it?"
Jeremiah 17:9

The troops are dismissed from evening colors to form chow lines at the steps of the mess hall. The boy in front moves quickly to get behind the Senior Patrol Leader and make sure that no one gets between them. He elbows everyone aside who threatens to get ahead of him in line. It makes absolutely no difference regarding how soon or how much he gets to eat. No one eats until all have taken their place at the tables and grace has been said. He just wants to be first. He will fight over the issue, if pressed.

Another boy is told repeatedly not to run in camp. It is explained that there are rocks and roots which threaten to trip and possibly injure anyone who breaks this rule. He has tripped and fallen while running at least once. He pays no attention and is seen to continue running even when an adult calls out to him to walk. Five minutes later he is running again.

Another boy, who is a close friend of several Scouts in the troop, is told repeatedly by his parents that he is not to skateboard in the streets. He is given specific instructions regarding what to do in the event his parents are not home when he gets home from school. Finding them not at home, he instead rides his skateboard into the street, into the pathway of an oncoming car. He is killed.

What is this thing in our nature, invisible to its owner but so readily apparent to others, that draws us into conflict and danger? Can it be understood? How may we deal with it? Boy Scouting is a veritable life observatory in which are seen almost unlimited behavioral examples reflecting the true nature of men. In boys it is more transparent, without the camouflage and varnish of older men, and Scouting is a wonderful opportunity to learn to deal with it.

C. S. Lewis describes the law of nature operating in man as one in which two facts may be observed: First, a moral law of right and wrong is generally understood and subscribed to by each man from within his heart, consistent across nations, races and religions. Second, each man expects others to observe the standards of the moral law but always seems to have excuses as to why it shouldn't apply to him regarding his particular actions. Every time he gives an excuse he acknowledges that he agrees with the moral law, else he would not devote such effort to justifying himself (either explaining his innocence or why he was exempt from obedience).*

Saint Paul also describes the operation of these laws of nature as they become visible in ourselves. He describes it as a war in which there is a law operating in his body which makes him unable to do what his mind agrees is right. He further explains that establishing rules, even the righteous commandments of the Bible, helps to reveal that there are laws operating in his flesh that will not keep these rules but that, instead, produce responses leading to death. "For I joyfully concur with the law of God in the inner man, but I see a different law in the members of my body, waging war against the law of my mind, and making me a prisoner of the law of sin which is in my members" (Rom. 7:22,23).

It is in every boy's nature to desire to be exalted, to be first, to have his own way and to cover his mistakes with whatever deception is required, because boys have the nature of the human race. But they are also malleable, teachable and able to capture a vision of what is right for their lives. They come to Scouting eager to be regarded as righteous and true, even if they bring little such commodity with them; with proper examples and teaching they can be brought to understand that it is actions, not words, which define their characters. We are to do our best to obey the Scout Law, rather than merely to say its words!

In order to comprehend the tremendous power men have to convey values and vision to boys and to change their behavior (in a family, in a Scouting program or any other similar program), it is useful to appreciate the means and extent to which people become bonded together when relationships become "load-bearing" and "life-giving." Bonding is essentially based on experientially giving out of one's own life into the life of another.

Scouting is essentially such an experiential program in which the transfer of knowledge to the Scouts is accomplished by the leader taking them into activities in which they learn by doing and where the leader pays an investment price into the life of each boy. His giving usually becomes unique and personal for each boy, because each is different and requires treatment as an individual. If the Scout is uncertain he can accomplish a particular outing requirement, such as hiking, survival or canoeing, he must be led into experiencing his own personal victory. He must therefore be fed "bite-sized" pieces of program that enable him to grow according to his capacity and that also gain his confidence that his capacities and limitations are appreciated by the leader.

On the other end of the exchange, as an experiential program, Scouting brings great strength to bear on the shaping of both a boy's skills and character. Practically everything that is taught gets rapid opportunity to be put into practice. Educators and trainers are aware that only about 20% of what we are taught verbally is retained the first time we hear it and that rapid application of even this is essential or it, too, will be lost. Scouts being given a good outdoor program will be immersed in repeated opportunities to establish and strengthen their skills and gain confidence in the instruction of their leaders. The greater the credibility of their leaders, the greater will be the Scouts' desire to emulate their character, as well.

The Scoutmaster also participates very directly in the Scouts' trials and tribulations. If it rains on the Scout, it also rains on the Scoutmaster. If the Scout is tired or hungry, the Scoutmaster shares the same ordeal. The Scout starts out assuming that the Scoutmaster knows nothing about his likes, dislikes, abilities or difficulties (and he assumes that when he talks about them, the Scoutmaster is hearing them all for the first time!). However, the fact that the Scoutmaster shares in the Scout's experience establishes a relationship. Participation is a leadership action on the part of the adult that affirms his commitment to the Scout, hence the value of the Scout as a person. If things fall short, the adult usually has the capacity to "pull it out of the bag," to complete what is needed to assure success. That counts until, with time, the Scout can look back and, in the context of the fun he has had, sense accomplishment in the things he has done and that the Scoutmaster is indeed his friend. Accomplishment breeds confidence that the Scoutmaster does understand his capabilities and limitations (and perhaps some other things, as well.) The credibility of the Scoutmaster increases according to the affirming experiences of the Scout.

It is important that a Scout not experience defeat. By "defeat," I mean serious debilitating damage, where the Scout's morale is so shattered, or the loss of face in front of his friends is so severe, or his spirit is so wounded that he cannot come back for another try. This is different from ordinary temporary set-backs, which are common and from which we all can spring up again to go on. Bad weather and bodily fatigue are the most frequent sources of sagging morale and it is important for the Scoutmaster to lead the boys through such experiences so that they taste the victory of a dry bed, warm meal and a good night's sleep on the other side of what they are going through. It is during these times that the Scoutmaster himself, also dog-tired, sweaty and insect bitten, must be most conscious of the impact of his actions upon Scouts that are looking to him for their encouragement and cues.

Scoutmasters can and will be manipulated by their Scouts, sometimes with maddening skill. It takes no time at all for a boy to figure out that if he delays in going to the bathroom, attending to a first aid matter or some such other priority item, he can get the whole group to wait for him after he has reclined, drunk out of his canteen and eaten his candies on the trail. He will soon be the one upon whom the party is always waiting, trying to sort out whether his pack is really improperly fitted, what is wrong with his socks or boots, figuring out why he is dizzy, or what have you. Eventually, when the Scoutmaster gets wise to the game, he must put his foot down or suffer the tyranny of the Scout, subjecting the goals of the entire group to his narrow, short-ranged issues of personal relief or gratification. In extreme cases, it is even possible to allow a boy to "defeat" himself by manipulating the Scoutmaster or another adult into carrying his pack or taking him home, thus incurring the scorn of his fellow Scouts.

However, until the Scoutmaster develops discernment, he should try to assure that any errors he makes favor mercy. He should allow himself to be manipulated if he is uncertain, and be gentle but firm in working through the discipline that he feels is necessary to achieve the group goals. It is precisely when the Scoutmaster is dog-tired, sweaty and insect bitten that he is most likely to become angry and impatient with a Scout and say something he may later regret. A boy can be led, but not forced or scorned. A boy named Nat once lay down on the trail and told me in tears he could go no further, triggering a severely scornful reply from me. I took part of his load and got him up the trail to the campsite, but I knew I had injured his spirit and was unwilling to apologize to him. He never came back to another troop meeting.

On another incident, a thunderstorm frightened a patrol camping in a small camping cabin in my yard and they came into the house to let it blow over. One boy snuck off a phone call to his dad to come and get him. When his dad showed up, no amount of reasoning or explanation to the father was successful in conveying the importance of the boy sticking it out with his patrol members. After the thunderstorm had passed, the father took his son home while the rest of the patrol went back out to the cabin and completed their weekend campout. The boy never came back to another Scout meeting.

With time the round-eyed, star-struck boy who comes into Scouting thinking the Scoutmaster walks on water and can do nothing wrong discovers that the Scoutmaster makes mistakes and that conflicts occur. However, by this time his fantasy should be replaced with relationships upon which he is confident and they will not suffer with the application of discipline. In fact, it is a good relationship with the adult leaders which supports discipline and draws the Scout through it successfully.

Contrary to the popular axiom that one should always compliment in public and reprove in private, there seems to be ample experience in Scouting to support the notion that there are certain situations where reproof in private is untimely or unproductive. Certain types of antisocial behavior by the Scout require immediate response as well as the Scout's accountability to all the leaders. Things that influence safety or group success or failure frequently require immediate correction of some action which has already been imposed upon the group by its instigator. Further, the Bible also teaches that repeat offenses are to be dealt with publicly to strengthen the effect of the discipline both on the offender and on others as well (Matt. 18:16-17, 1 Tim. 5:20).

Does this discussion mean that Scouting can accomplish fundamental behavioral change by changing the nature of a boy? No, I don't believe that it can. As the boy grows older and has the advantage of repeatedly enforced standards and maturity, he can outgrow childish behavior and improve his capacity to do what is right both individually and in society. His character and citizenship can be developed. But the fundamental drives of his nature to promote himself over others, to reject the guidance or discipline of authority in favor of his own reasoning will remain unchanged — unless his nature is changed. I believe, rather, that Scouting can provide good moral leadership which reinforces what the conscience, the internally written moral law in each boy's heart, is already saying to each individual Scout, which he agrees to be right. He can become accustomed to seeing right examples in action in the lives of his adult leaders. He can become accustomed to being held accountable for his actions when he falls short while discovering that falling short is not the end of the world to those who love him. By this means he can be assisted in seeing that there is, indeed, a war in his members between what he knows to be right and would like to do and what he may frequently do instead. This reinforces the truth and may open him up eventually to the knowledge of his need for help which goes beyond his own strength. Hence, Scouting can potentially serve as a useful instrument in demonstrating the truth of what the Bible teaches and prepare him for the gospel of Jesus Christ, who can change his nature.

---

* C.S. Lewis, *Mere Christianity*, Macmillan Publishing Co., NY

28

Salvation

"...To whom has the arm of the Lord been revealed?"
                                                    Isaiah 53:1

The telephone rang in the middle of the night. As I struggled awake and turned on the light, I noticed it was 2:00 a.m. Sleepily, I answered the phone.

"Mr. Duff, it's me, Russ! Guess what? I met the Lord and I've been saved!" Russ was calling me long distance from Seattle, not realizing there is a three-hour time difference between Seattle and Alexandria. He had just come from a date with his girlfriend, who had led him to Christ. It was apparent that he had had a very vivid salvation experience and was eager to share it.

"I used to wonder what you were talking about when you spoke of 'The Lord' all the time. Now I know! Wow! This is amazing! What a surprise to find out that Jesus is really alive!" Russ went on for over an hour giving me a blow-by-blow account of how God had answered his prayer to receive Christ with clear evidence of His power and reality. It was a rich time of sharing. It was Russ's father who years earlier had been healed of a broken back through prayer (described in an earlier chapter of this book). Russ himself had come into the Scout troop at the advanced age of 14, full of rebellion and a need to express himself over the younger boys who all knew more than he did about Scouting and outdoor skills. I had been uncertain at the time whether or not to encourage him to stay in Scouting, because of his advanced age, and had warned him that he could expect to get out of Scouting what he put into it. He made a conscious decision to stay and in the space of little over three years made Life Scout. We have kept in touch through his period of service in the Navy and marriage (to the girl who led him to Christ), over ten years.

Many are the incidents in which God has moved in personal ways to meet Scouts and ex-Scouts with demonstrated proof of His reality and love for them, and many have come to Christ. Few are the specific moments where I can recall ever consciously witnessing or speaking to them about Christ, with the exception of Sunday morning devotional services while on campouts. There have been difficult campout situations where prayer has taken place and occasions around campfires where the story telling has produced testimony of great things which God has done in our Scout troops. Woven into the fabric of my own life has been whatever I am living at the moment, either in or out of Christ. The Scouts have had ample opportunity to see me as I am without my being conscious of it.

One humiliating experience in which God proved Himself to us was on the occasion of a bicycle trip on the C&O Canal from Washington, D.C. to Harper's Ferry, Virginia. We had not gone far from downtown Georgetown when Max, another adult leader, lost one of his contact lenses. Almost from the start of our search, the Lord told me we would not find it unless we stopped and prayed for it.

It was a Saturday and there were hundreds of people walking and riding to and fro on the canal path. The path had crushed gravel on it and we were down on our hands and knees looking for the lens. I resisted the urging of the Lord and persisted in the search. He repeated the admonition. Again I resisted.

However, I tightened up the discipline of search, giving each person one lineal foot of the path and having us proceed two inches at a time in a line abreast of 10 or so boys as we carefully searched the area where Max knew his contact lens to have fallen out. I cannot reconstruct why it seemed more humiliating to me to face the prospect of public prayer together than to continue our process of creeping along on our hands and knees with our fannies sticking up in the air, looking for the lense!

Finally, after about twenty minutes of this, The Lord really impressed it upon me: "Karl, you will not find this lens unless you commit it to Me through public prayer with these boys." Very reluctantly, since I really doubted that God would deliver on His implied promise to find the lens if we did pray, I called the boys together and told them what God had told me. Then we prayed. Out loud and together, we asked God to return to us the lens and thanked Him for it. Then we returned to our hands and knees crawling through the crushed gravel which by this time had been trodden by the feet of many dozens of people, as well as ourselves. I began to realize that if we did find it, it would be scratched beyond repair and recalled that God had not said in what condition we might recover the lens.

For fully another half hour we labored in vain, while I struggled with the prospects of giving up after having committed prayer to the issue. Finally, though, with the day wearing away, we had to continue our bicycle journey. I called it quits. We got up and returned to our bicycles. As we were getting on, Max happened to look down and cried out, "Hey, look! My contact lens stuck to the crossbar on my bicycle!"

Sure enough, there it was, in perhaps the only safe place it could possibly have been, while we pummeled the ground looking for it.

God-led incidents like this may have something to do with Scouts later coming to know Christ. But I doubt there is any formula or pattern which can be "boxed" or described. God is intent on establishing His own personal relationship with each person of His creation, and no man will package it or successfully imitate it.

One thing, though, gives me encouragement. At one stage in my walk with Christ and in Boy Scouting, I used to get up early in the morning and pray for each Scout by name and for his family — for salvation and other blessings. One morning the Lord spoke to me and, in addition to perhaps letting me know that I was overdoing it, gave me this assurance: "Karl, be assured that every boy who comes into this Scout troop will be given a personal knowledge of Jesus Christ and will be saved!"

A promise like this is so amazing and incredible that I hesitate to share it. It is still unfulfilled. But God promised it to me with an assurance that passes all understanding. Someday I will see it and be satisfied (Is. 53:11).

Boy Scouts Live in the Supernatural!

138 LORD AND SCOUTMASTER

Boy Scouts Live in the Supernatural!

29

Strength Out of Adversity

"And after you have suffered for a little while, the God of all grace, who called you to His eternal glory in Christ, will Himself perfect, confirm, strengthen and establish you."
First Peter 5:10

You could tell that Damion was an unusually bright boy from the first moment you met him. At his Webelos "Crossing Over" ceremony into Boy Scouts, he enjoyed demonstrating his knowledge, his precocious reading and wide set of interests. He was the eldest son of his family and obviously motivated to achieve. I anticipated that he would blaze an aggressive path to Eagle Scout.

There was, however, another unusual trait to Damion. He seemed to be depressed and negative in his attitudes to an extreme degree. He complained about everything. A normal conversation with him would usually open like this;

"Hi, Damion! How are you?"

"Well, not so good. I've been feeling poorly ever since I got up this morning. My head's been bothering me and everything I've been doing today seems to be going wrong." Five, six, ten conversations in a row would go like this.

I soon became alert to this negative spirit and tried to avoid asking questions which would invite him to tell me all of the things that were going wrong in his life, but it was unavoidable. Every circumstance seemed to be designed to defeat Damion. He could discern it and express it no matter how positive the countervailing attitudes were. He wore it on his sleeve and it would not be denied. It was depressing.

I began to speak to him about it and tried to illustrate to him some of his statements so that he could see how they came across as negative, also creating a negative effect on listeners as well as on some of the efforts we were trying to accomplish. This had little effect. He seemed to understand intellectually, but it appeared that it was his actual attitude that was creating the problem. Words wouldn't change his spirit. He actually was negative in his outlook and an intellectual appreciation of the situation would not change his view of himself or his perceived problems.

This continued for about six months, by which time I was praying for Damion and asking God to rid him from this negative spirit. I made special efforts to keep conversation with Damion very positive in tone and tried not to allow his negative outlook on things to affect our discussions or decisions, but continued to see no progress. Then I became more strident in my prayers. I resolved that I wanted God to rid Damion of this negative spirit.

Near the end of Damion's first year in Boy Scouting, we took the troop skiing up in Pennsylvania. The ski slope was about three hours' drive from Washington, D.C. Following several hours of ski instruction at the bottom of the slopes, we released the Scouts to ski on the easiest of the "bunny" hills. On my first ride up the chair lift, I watched Damion come down the hill, saw his skis come apart and him fall between his skis. He didn't move. Although we had never previously experienced a serious skiing injury with Scouts, I seemed to know at once that this was serious.

I got to Damion in a few moments, by which time the ski patrol was already on its way. We got him to the ski patrol hut and it was obvious that Damion had broken a leg. They administered first aid, put on a leg splint and helped get him into my car for the drive into Harrisburg and a hospital for medical treatment. I also notified his parents and kept them informed with the progress of x-rays, summoning an off-duty doctor to come in and set the leg, place the cast, and so on. As it was a Saturday, it required an inordinately long time; the afternoon was over by the time I called to report completion of the medical treatment. Now we had to resolve the major problem that had been creeping up on us all day.

It was obvious that we needed to get Damion home. One would not normally think of any other alternative after treatment for a broken leg for a young boy. Damion wanted to go home. However, it was not that easy. I was Scoutmaster of the troop, responsible for the rest of the campout and a troop now facing evening meal preparation at a nearby Boy Scout camp. It was a six-hour round trip either for me to drive Damion to Alexandria or for his parents to come up and get him. Meeting at an intermediate point would still require a three-hour drive for each of us. The weather was somewhat threatening and that much time on the road in poor weather was not attractive to either his parents or me. On the other hand, the cabin the troop was staying in had electric lights and a wood stove for heating, together with bunks and mattresses for sleeping. If Damion could be persuaded ... hmm. His parents and I began to discuss the possibility of Damion's remaining with the troop overnight.

As we began to discuss the possibility, the scene began to take on new dimensions. Damion would have to be an assenting partner to the decision. What kind of an appeal could we make to him? What could he find attractive in staying overnight, when every fiber in his 12-year-old body cried to go home? Then other dim lights began to come on in my mind. We would be coming into direct confrontation with the most resolute aspects of Damion's attitude toward adverse circumstances. Could he be persuaded to an action that would place him over his circumstances rather than the other way round? We decided to give it a try.

It was not easy. Damion had good reasons and strong emotions opting for home — and old habits do not die easily, either. But there is reality, too, in wanting to experience victory. We acknowledge in the tradition of placing signatures on plaster casts that there is a mild form of homage to the injured. But that is only vestigial homage compared to that given heroes in battle who prevail, though wounded! Merely having your cast signed cannot compare with camping out in your new cast with the boys who came skiing with you, without even going home!

We talked with the doctor about it, considered that Damion would have some pain pills for the first day or two, painted pictures of dinner and breakfast in bed, no chores and the Scouts waiting on the injured victor. The prospects began to look pretty good to Damion. He decided to spend the night and go home the next day with the Scout troop.

It was a piece of cake! Damion was carried in on a stretcher, enthroned on his bunk, treated like the royalty he was and required only his first pain pill. He awoke once in the night with some discomfort and slept the rest of the night like a baby. When we left the next day, his stretcher had become a royal litter.

A remarkable change began to be visible in Damion. He became an overcomer! No longer did circumstances easily overwhelm him. No longer did personal discomfort seem to be too great a price to pay for accomplishing an important objective. Obstacles could be overcome if he made up his mind. As an example, the following year, while on a High Adventure Trip in New Hampshire, Damion decided to climb from our base camp on the north side of 6288-feet. Mt. Washington (the tallest mountain in New England) to its summit and back on two successive days, a seven-mile round trip, merely because he had not purchased a commemorative cloth patch at the top on the first day! Later, he hiked over the summit of Mt. Jefferson with a full pack when a majority of the troop hiked around it!

Like trees that develop strong roots when blown by strong winds, so men develop strength when subjected to adversity. Far be it from me to claim that the Lord responded to my prayers with a broken leg for Damion! Yet He helped us help Damion to overcome it, and in so doing changed something deep in Damion's spirit.

Damion had a dickens of a time focusing on achieving Life Scout. Four required merit badges and circumstances seemed to stand forever against him. But he overcame them. Now Damion is closing in on Eagle Scout. Circumstances still conspire to thwart him. But now he knows in his heart he can overcome his circumstances. He has demonstrated it repeatedly.

Seeds of Baden-Powell

"...Look toward the heavens and count the stars, if you are able to count them....So shall your descendents be."
Genesis 15:5

The above promise was given to Abraham by God when He called him to be a father of nations and father of faithful believers. God told him that in his obedience, He would make Abraham a blessing to nations.

Scouting is an apt analogy in that it has produced millions of men who, to various degrees, contain the good seed planted by its founder, Lord Baden-Powell of Great Britain. A good look at Baden-Powell's life and beliefs is inspirational and informative.

In the forward of his autobiography, *Lessons of a Lifetime*, Lord Baden-Powell says: "Almost any biography will have its useful suggestions for making life a success, but none better or more unfailing than the biography of Christ."

It may come as a surprise to many to discover that Lord Baden-Powell, a full-fledged adventurer and the founder of the Boy Scout movement, was also a believing Christian who not only frequently expressed his faith in God, His beauty and nature, but particularly recognized the difference between religion and Christianity. Even in the conservative British writing style typical of 55 years ago, his faith in God and in Jesus Christ is evident by his own testimony.

He was also a man talented almost beyond belief. The son of a clergyman, he developed skills as an artist (illustrating his own autobiography), sculptor, bandmaster and musician (violin and horn), actor and comic. He was also a soldier whose incredible adventures over the face of the globe ran a gamut of game-hunting and "one-upsmanship" contests with his army and native counterparts (in true 19th-century British style) to a multitude of solid accomplishments that won him world renown and promotion to Lieutenant General by the age of fifty.

His views regarding the building of manhood and citizenship are those which were imprinted upon Scouting, which are testified of within these pages and in Scouting today.

He found the public schools deficient in the development of character and in "attributes needed for making reliable men." In training soldiers he learned to take them back to nature and backwoodsmanship principles

"...the primitive, to learn tracking, eye for a country, observation by night as well as by day, to learn to stalk and to hide, to improvise shelter and to feed and fend for themselves..." He found that something more than actual ability and value as army Scouts was incidentally brought about. "One found that they had gained a measure of pride in their work, confidence in themselves, and a sense of responsibility and trust and other qualities such as put them on to a higher standard of manliness, self-respect and loyalty." He spoke frequently of the need to inculcate a "spirit of adventure," pluck, intelligence and initiative not found in school books. He noticed that many men were lost through desertion when placed in the boredom of regular barracks life and drill, whereas when placed in such a training program, desertion was "very rare indeed."

It was these observations and convictions that led to his writing of the book *Scouting for Boys*. They led also to his testing and confirming its concepts at Brownsea Island prior to its publication, launching the Boy Scouting movement.

Hearkening back to his own boyhood, which involved a good deal of sea-going work with his brothers, he realized the "extraordinary value of this training. It brought out various qualities which no amount of land-training could produce to the same extent. Apart from the bodily health developed, it familiarized the lad with risks and hardships incident to seafaring in all weathers, and demanded of him the exercise of courage and caution, coupled with discipline, self-reliance and resource, etc., all of which tended to make a man of him."

Baden-Powell then goes on to say, "In these days of modern coddling and the cult of 'safety first' Sea Scouting can give something of the hardiness badly needed in the make-up of a modern man." It was on this basis that Sea Scouting was founded.

Also contained within his autobiography are thoughts regarding success in life and happiness. In Baden-Powell's view the two words are nearly synonymous and the secret of gaining happiness is by "happifying," the two paramount needs being the building of a happy marriage and the rendering of service to others in the community. "Without this, the mere satisfaction of selfish desire does not reach the top notch."

By the nature of his life, Baden-Powell was able to plant and reproduce his own good seed in millions of other men. I am among those who have seen for themselves that the principles which he learned and passed on are true. I have myself become an heir and beneficiary of his life, although for many years I didn't know who he was.

The same is true of Jesus and what He has done for me and for all mankind. For many years I didn't know who He was. Yet to all who receive Him, He gives the right to become "children of God, even to those who believe in His name" (John 1:12). He gave His life for us, that we might have eternal life. He set the example of life-giving for us. Baden-Powell followed His example, even resigning from the army at the peak of his career to devote himself full-time to Boy Scouting.

We who are the heirs must continue to work to reproduce the good seed that Jesus, the Son of God, and His servant Lord Baden-Powell have placed in us.

31

The Nowhere Road

This story was told at an evening campfire to spellbound Scouts by Mr. Ronsevald, Camp Parsons, Washington Camp Director, in 1949.

In the mountains of the southeastern United States are some of the most densely wooded and remote forests of our country. Giant rhododendrons and mountain laurel grow under a canopy of oaks, maples and hickory up steep hillsides that rise from deep river canyons and guard the flanks of huge mountains nearly 7000 feet tall. The tops of these mountains are covered with almost impenetrable evergreen stands of balsam fir and red spruce. Travel is very difficult; yet from the earliest days of our country, a few brave souls ventured into and explored these mountains. Many never came back.

One particular region near where the border of Tennessee and North Carolina is now located had a particularly large and rugged area of high mountains where travel was very difficult and development of civilization was slow. Only a few small collections of mountaineers nestled near the foot of these mountains and it was only for purposes of hunting or fishing that a few woodsmen went further back into the hills. The hills were too rugged to clear for livestock and so the mountains stayed essentially as they had been for centuries, dark and foreboding.

Over a period of several hundred years, starting from before the American Revolution, a certain legend grew among the people that there was a mysterious road hidden somewhere in those mountains that led to nowhere. No one knew this for certain, but there were well-founded stories of men who had gone into the mountains and not returned. These were experienced outdoorsmen who were quite capable of taking care of themselves against accident or wild animals as well as finding their way into the mountains and back.

There was no easy explanation as to why these men had simply disappeared, never to be seen again. The legends of the early Indian tribes in the area had also recounted the same story of one or two brave Indian warriors who had disappeared into the mountains. It was the Indians who had first told of a road that led to nowhere. Once a person found it, he could never return. This legend came to be called "The Legend of the Nowhere Road."

Shortly after the turn of this century, a prisoner escaped from the state penitentiary and fled from pursuing police into these mountains. He was sighted at a distance by a few of the mountaineers as he fled up one of the river valleys and into the deep forests. When the police came, they were warned by the local people that they would be best advised not to try to follow the convict lest they risk being lost themselves on the "Nowhere Road." A few of the police followed anyway until they became so confused and frightened in the wilderness that they were forced to turn around and find their way back out again. But the convict was never seen or heard of again.

About twenty years after this incident, a young newspaperman from one of the towns near the Atlantic coast came to these mountains to obtain some information for a story he wanted to write on the local inhabitants of the region. He was intrigued by the mountaineers and wanted to capture some of their color and strange habits by spending some time among them. He made arrangements to rent a small room over the general store and began to try to get to know some of the people. Since he was a stranger, this took a little time, but after awhile a few of them invited him to share at their dinner table, and it was not much longer before he first began to hear the tales of the Nowhere Road. He was immediately fascinated and wanted to find out as much as he could.

However, no matter how much he asked, he couldn't find anyone who really knew whether or not such a road actually existed. No one had actually gone into the mountains to look for it. He concluded that the local people were prisoners of superstition and fear and that it would be good for him to try to search out the truth of the matter himself. He was somewhat experienced as a woodsman and soon gathered the necessary supplies, hiking boots and rucksack that he needed to spend several days in the mountains exploring.

On the day of his departure, the local inhabitants again urged him to give up his idea of looking for the Nowhere Road, but his mind was made up. He started up the little wagon road that led to the last few houses in the hollow and soon found himself alone. The wagon road turned into a trail. Within an hour or so it was evident that the trail was mostly used by the deer and other wild animals. The woods also seemed to be getting much darker.

As he worked his way deeper into the mountains, the young newspaperman noticed that the bushes seemed to get thicker, also. The trail narrowed and the bushes began to pull at his clothes as he forced his way up the steep slope. Sweat soaked his clothes and he had to stop more often to rest. Soon the trail disappeared altogether. He had a strong sense of foreboding, as though he were in danger, but he reminded himself that he was not superstitious as were the local mountaineers and that there was nothing to fear. He had food and supplies for several days and it would be quite simple to find his way back down the valley to the town, once he decided to return. When darkness came, he found a small campsite, built a fire just large enough to drive back the dark shadows and slept fitfully during the night, waking up before the sun rose.

As he continued up the hills into the mountains the next morning, the man noticed that things had gradually grown more quiet. He no longer could hear the roar of the large stream pouring down the valley, and the air seemed to hang quietly in the trees, as though expecting something to happen. The slope of the ground gradually began to ease and he noticed also that the trees were not as large as they had been. There were more spruce and fir trees now in place of the deciduous trees. Although the going began to get somewhat easier, his sense of concern also began to increase. He had been traveling for a day now and had not yet reached a top of a ridge. He had no idea exactly where he was and he began to doubt that he could retrace his steps exactly as he had come up the valley. He began to break twigs and leave other trail signs that would help him find his way back.

He stopped near noon for a short snack and, finding that half of his rations were gone, began to realize that he would have to turn back if he did not make some discovery before long. Although the travel had been difficult, there was certainly nothing in the country he had traveled thus far that would prevent experienced Indians or mountaineers from finding their way back to civilization. Still, he persisted up the hill, now noticeably easier as the evergreen trees began to grow thicker and thicker. It became more difficult to tell by which route he had come, and he broke yet more twigs as he went along to assure he would be able to find his way back. He had the feeling he was getting close to the top of something and that if he could only continue for a short while longer, he would satisfy his desire to at least get to the top of the ridge and gain a view of the surrounding country. At the same time his concern increased that he might really be extending himself beyond his supplies and ability to find his way back.

As the afternoon progressed the young man's concern reached critical levels. He had just decided that it would be foolish to continue any further and it was time to turn back when he noticed an opening in the trees ahead. Surely, once he reached that opening he would be able to get some kind of a view! So he continued on a few hundred yards to where the trees parted and he stepped onto a partially open grassy area in the midst of the trees. The area was quite flat on the ridge top, extending both to his left and his right. But he could see that off to his right a little point on the ridge seemed to rise up where he would be able to get a better view. So he continued on a short way further to see what the view would reveal. When he came to this point, he could see that the clearing he was following extended up the ridge to an even higher point where the views would be even better. He decided to continue a bit longer. At the next point he noticed another just a bit higher and with better views and he went on again. This happened several more times.

As he walked along from point to point, the way now being quite easy, he began again to feel the hair on his neck rise. What was he being drawn into? Like a magnet, he felt himself being drawn from one point to the next along this open pathway, always seeking a better view. Suddenly he realized, "I must be on the Nowhere Road! The stories must be true. I need to turn back now." He saw one more high point about a half mile ahead which seemed to tower over the countryside and decided that once he gained the view from that spot he would definitely turn back. The grass turned to rock as he continued to climb along the ridge.

Ascending the last few feet toward the top of the last rocky point, the newspaperman saw the countryside open up as the views extended in all directions. The very top was a large flat rock. Gazing out as he stepped onto it, the rock suddenly tipped and he found himself falling. Everything turned black!

Splash! He had only fallen about 30 feet when he suddenly found himself immersed in a deep pool of water. The weight of his boots and rucksack was dragging him to the bottom. He struggled to get the rucksack off his back. The straps were too tight; they seemed stuck to his body. Finally he tore it off. Then he swam with all his might for the surface. His lungs were bursting as he finally broke the surface of the water, gasping for breath. He took off his boots and let them drop to the bottom. Then he began to explore the walls of his pool in the darkness. His heart sank as he realized that the walls of the cistern into which he had fallen were vertical, smooth rock! It would be only a matter of time until he drowned.

As he gathered his wits and began to calm down somewhat, he commenced a more methodical exploration of the walls with his hands, seeking some possible small handholds where he might be able to hang on for awhile. Reaching up as far as he could reach, he discovered a small ledge where he was able to place one hand and then the other. Not feeling any backside to the ledge, he decided to try and lift himself up onto it. Gathering all his strength, he pulled with all his might and mantled himself up onto the ledge on his belly where he lay there gasping. He had not drowned, after all. Perhaps there was a chance he could survive awhile on this ledge.

Now he began to explore with his hands. He was horror-stricken to feel bones scattered all over the ledge. Thinking for a few moments, he realized that he still had a few paraffin-coated matches in his shirt pocket. He lit one and looked around.

The ledge was about eight feet long and four feet wide, tapering at both ends. On it were the bones of five or six men. One was extremely old and had a skull with a sloping forehead. One was bare except for small scraps of leather and a few beads and animal teeth which had once been bracelets or necklaces. Two had bones which were covered by moldy layers of old buckskin. The most recent one was covered with the black and white stripes of prison garb. Here was the final resting place of those who had found the Nowhere Road! The newspaperman struck another match and investigated further. Scattered among the bones were old worn down utensils, flints and knives. In the back of the ledge an inscription had been scraped into the rock, which he was able to make out. Next to it were a series of steps that started up the vertical wall. The first was crude and irregular, about 2 feet up from the ledge. The next was slightly improved, about 2 feet further up. Above those were several more.

The newspaperman searched his remaining belongings. His only tool was a folding pocket knife. He climbed the steps as far as he could, holding on with his left hand and began scraping at the rock with the steel blade of his pocket knife.

Chip by chip, working in the pitch blackness, he could feel the rock beginning to give way under the blade of the knife. As his arm would tire and begin to cramp, he would shift to his other hand, continuing to work at the rock. One inch, two inches, three inches; deeper went the step. But as the step went deeper, slower went the progress. For the pocket knife was also wearing down and so was the newspaperman. His food was gone and much effort was required to hang on the wall while carving the step. His rest periods became longer and longer; first minutes, then hours. His fingers became bloody and the periods of time when he could climb up and work on the step became shorter and shorter. His body became emaciated and weak. Exhaustion came and he finally lay down on the ledge for the last time. The knife was worn down to the handle. He could carve no more.

The newspaperman lay there considering his final resting place with the others with whom he shared his fate. It made no difference that he had not listened to the warnings. He had needed to find the truth. Now he was joined to the others. He drifted slowly off to sleep.

Suddenly there came a flash of light and a scream! Down through the darkness came another tumbling body and a splash in the pool. The newspaper man regained some of his senses and crawled to the edge of the ledge as a man came spluttering to the surface of the pool. Shouting to him, he reached out his hand and helped him out of the water and onto the ledge.

The man who had just fallen into the pool was a member of a rescue party, sent out to look for the newspaper man. When he hadn't returned after a few days, the town had contacted the newspaper company and told them of what he had done. The company organized a well-equipped party who had little trouble following the newspaperman and his series of broken branches and trail signs. The man who had fallen in was the first to arrive at the rocky summit with the tilt stone.

In a few minutes others arrived who had seen the mishap. Soon they had successfully rescued both men from the cistern. Subsequent efforts permanently fixed the summit rock so that never again would anyone fall into the cistern.

What was the inscription which the newspaperman read on the wall?
"Carve your step. Help those who follow."

Epilogue

Portent for Scouting's Future

"But whoever shall deny Me before men, I will also deny him before My Father who is in heaven."

Matthew 10:33

Changes are coming to Boy Scouting. Powerful forces are working today both within the program itself and within the lives of the boys who live their formative teenage years under its leadership and teaching. The effects we see are not auspicious, but shed light on the way we should go. There is a desperate need for leadership willing to stand in defense of youth, especially the young men upon whom depends the future safety of families and of the nation.

Until recently, most changes in Scouting seemed to be of a nature which reflected only upon the relative judgments of the leadership involved, their understanding of boys and their vision for Scouting. There has remained plenty of room to accommodate ranges of opinion which have not jeopardized basic tenets.

Things have changed now, however. Since 1987, dramatic changes in the legal and philosophical position of the Boy Scouts of America have taken place which reflect the times in which we live.

In 1987 a lawsuit was filed against the Boy Scouts of America on behalf of a Scout who was denied approval for his Eagle award by his Eagle Board of Review due to the fact that he professed not to believe in God, declaring instead that he was an atheist. It is noted that each Scout and Scouter pledge upon entering Scouting to "do their best" to support the Scout Law, which contains as its 12th point that "A Scout is Reverent." Under this point, the explanation is provided in the *Boy Scout Handbook*: "A Scout is reverent toward God. He is faithful in his religious duties. He respects the beliefs of others."

Discussion in the Scout Handbook has been gradually watered down over the years to reduce (and then to remove) reference to "worship of God". Until the 1990 revision of the *Boy Scout Handbook*, however, the discussion still left no doubt that we are called upon to place our trust in God and "work within His plan," while respecting the religions of others who worship God in a different way. The most recent edition, however, has further watered this down to remove any concept of a personal God that can be "trusted" and refers instead to God only in the context of being visible in the "mysteries of the universe" and the "kindness of people." It deletes any reference to worship and explains showing reverence only in the context of one living one's life "according to the ideals of our beliefs." This is now clearly a relativistic and humanistic philosophy that no longer postulates a personal, trustworthy God. It also places all other forms of nonbelief and relativistic philosophy on equal footing. It can now be said that the spirit of a personal, living God is dead in the *Boy Scout Handbook*.

The outcome of the lawsuit was that the Boy Scouts of America agreed to an out-of-court settlement and granted the atheist his Eagle award.

An earlier chapter pointed out the steady trend of reduction in the number of fathers who are able or willing to spend time Scouting, imparting their skills, character and knowledge to boys. One of the accompanying trends (or results) of this is that women are insisting on doing it themselves, perhaps little realizing the full significance of their position. Shortly after the settlement of the lawsuit mentioned above, the Boy Scouts of America, after winning a court case on the issue, changed another of their policies of nearly 80 years and now permit women Scoutmasters.

A surge in lawsuits against the Boy Scouts of America for injury to Scouts while on Scouting activities has caused a dramatic increase in the cost of liability insurance for Scout Troops and leaders. This coverage is provided by the Scouting program as a feature of its chartering each of its units through annual registration. The result is that the cost of a unit charter and of joining the Scouting program has more than tripled in only a few years and continues to increase.

The most recent sign of the times which has come against Boy Scouting and our nation is the occurrence of sexual abuse by men who have used Scouting to gain access to young boys. The effects have been insidious, ranging from much more stringent lines of accountability in background verification of all new Scouters to no longer permitting any Scout leader to have one-on-one access to a Scout. All instruction, counselling, Scoutmaster's conferences and merit badge work must now include a third party. This has the effect of requiring Scouts who are going to a merit badge counsellor's home for sign-off of a merit badge to take another Scout or parent with them. The policy of background verification is all-inclusive, including even those who have only remote association with the Scouts themselves (i.e., Scouting Coordinators, Sponsoring Institution Heads, etc.). Since Scouting is a volunteer activity, it seems likely that these new policies, necessitated by the moral disintegration of our society, will have the effect of further discouraging otherwise qualified men from volunteering to work as unit leaders or merit badge counsellors; it will discourage those who are not already strongly motivated from becoming associated with Scouting.

Past changes, introduced over a longer period, perhaps deserve now to be accorded more sociological significance than they were at the time. Lowering the minimum age for Boy Scouts first from age 12 to age 11, then to 10½ (for those who have finished the fifth grade), was more than tacit recognition that the interests, knowledge levels and even physical maturity of our nation's youth were changing and fewer of them were entering Scouting. Efforts of Scouting to "capture" or retain a larger portion of the male youth is reflected in the introduction in 1980 of Varsity Scouting, which attempts to cater to the desire of increasing numbers of boys to engage in competitive sports at the expense of the other types of activity programs of Boy Scouting and Explorer Scouting. The struggle to attract and retain boys has now reached the extreme of introducing Tiger Cubs, which allows boys to enter Scouting at age seven! In 1988, the Webelos "transition" program from Cub Scouting to Boy Scouting was increased from one to two years. Yet the "burn-out" of both Cub Scouts and their parents, causing them to shun Boy Scouting, continues unabated and will potentially increase. The percentage of teenage boys in Scouting is still decreasing.

But other evidence is accumulating that even stronger forces are at work. These forces in our society are fast overtaking and destroying even youth who have been successful in Scouting. Drugs, sexual promiscuity, the occult and unfaithfulness in employment and marriage are ripping the lives of young men for whom the work of their parents and the efforts of Scouting have not been sufficient to build successful men. There are more and more young men in our society today (some mentioned in the pages of this book) who are now in bondage, who beat their wives, can't hold a job, are alcoholic or are in other such forms of extreme bondage that they are unable to lead successful lives or raise up successful families. I grieve over their helplessness and destruction. Where is trustworthiness? Where is faithfulness? Where is the cleanliness and character, set forth in the Scout Law before them for years? Is it not evident that there is something still missing in the successful building of true manhood in our young men? It is Jesus, the Hope of our Salvation, the very Essence of manhood, who is so often missing!

The 1990 edition of the *Boy Scout Handbook* has been rewritten to address some of these subjects, such as child abuse and substance abuse. No doubt this will assist in reducing the danger to youth having parents who care for them and take the new guidelines to heart. But the *Handbook* further removes trust and worship of God as a central precept. How sufficient will this prove? For example, how successful will the guidelines be to reducing the life-damaging effects of sexual promiscuity that are ravaging the lives of so many of our youth today? How successful will any approach be that presumes our youth and our nation face a secular problem rather than one which is spiritual?

Our nation has had prior issues upon which minorities took unpopular positions of conscience regarding its future course (i.e., independence, slavery, prohibition, minority rights, etc.). These issues each tore the fabric of our nation in their time. However, never has there been such a host of issues relating to the life and health of our nation's ability to raise families. Drugs, sexual immorality, pornography and perversion, the slaughter of unborn babies, witchcraft, teenage suicides and the wholesale rampage of child abuse and divorce all reflect upon the advanced state of destruction of the American male and with him, his wives and children.

As a result, there is an emergent theme of increasing national political conflict between those who hold that the Bible contains trustworthy behavioral standards and solutions for these problems and those who don't. The lines are becoming more and more distinct and the middle ground is shrinking. Boy Scouting, whether it realizes it or not, is being pressed into the midst of the conflict. There is a war going on and Scouting is currently involved in it — and losing.

"...I would that you were cold or hot. So because you are lukewarm, and neither hot nor cold, I will spit you out of My mouth" (Rev. 3:15,16). Such are the words of Jesus to the members of His Church who cling to a lukewarm commitment to Him. Can the situation be any different for Scouting, or any other secular institution that professes the existence of God, but denies His power? (2 Tim. 3:5)

It is possible that we are observing a sifting and sorting process, already commenced in our society and in the world, which will become more evident and accelerate with time prior to the return of Jesus. In His teaching, Jesus referred to the need for men to acknowledge Him as "He whom the Father has sent" (John 8:19-29), "The way, the truth, and the life" (John 14:6) without whom no one comes to the Father. He taught that those who deny Him before the world He will also deny before the Father in heaven (Matt. 10:33), and that at Judgment He will separate the sheep from the goats (Matt. 25:32-46) with the declaration that He never knew "many" who used His name (Matt. 7:22,23).

Possibly Scouting has been in the middle ground all along, and not realized it. Perhaps men who originally knew the Author of their foundational precepts can pass them to successors who do not; but then how can precepts, segregated from their author, long survive by themselves? Now pressure has caused Scouting to begin to abandon its basic precepts, upon which the Scout Oath and Law are founded. It has given atheism equal footing with those who profess to believe in God. (Would Lord Baden-Powell, who professed the Lord Jesus Christ, have approved?) It has abandoned the precept that the seed of manhood must be given to boys by men and cannot be given by women. It is being assailed from all sides by struggles with finances, liability suits, perversion and loss of membership.

The precepts of Scouting will certainly survive somewhere! They are founded in the truth of the Word of God. They give life to boys as well as to men; they instill vision, right standards, accountability and some degree of the character contained in the twelve Scout Laws. They convey values regarding right and wrong and some motivation to pay the price of doing right. But it is possible that only those who know that God is alive and has power to uphold His precepts in the lives of those who confess Him will be able to sustain the precepts of Scouting in the coming years. If true, it implies that the productive future of Scouting lies within the body (the Church) of Jesus Christ and under the leadership of men who profess Christ as the true Author of Scouting's precepts. Deliverance of our youth will require placing more rather than less emphasis on the message of salvation in Jesus Christ. It will require placing the holy Scriptures and prayer alongside of adventure in building citizenship, character and physical fitness in boys, the spirit of Scouting being nurtured in a seed bed that is "hot" rather than "lukewarm."

Who will answer the call? "Who has believed our report and to whom has the arm of the Lord been revealed?" (Is. 53:1) Who will build his step, yielding his life to the service of boys even while, in unexplainable ways, he also receives it back again?

"...But where sin increased, grace abounded all the more" (Rom. 5:20). God will not leave the prayers of His children unanswered! Nor will Christ allow His flock to be destroyed by hirelings. He will certainly raise up men to answer the call.